What Happened to the Dinosaurs, Mastodons, and Dodo Birds?

EXTINCTION

with 25 Projects

LAURA PERDEW

Illustrated by Tom Casteel

~ More life science titles in the *Build It Yourself* series ~

Check out more titles at www.nomadpress.net

Nomad Press
A division of Nomad Communications
10 9 8 7 6 5 4 3 2 1

This book was manufactured by Versa Press
East Peoria, Illinois
September 2017, Job #J17-06476

ISBN Softcover: 978-1-61930-561-8
ISBN Hardcover: 978-1-61930-557-1

Educational Consultant, Marla Conn

Questions regarding the ordering of this book should be addressed to
Nomad Press
2456 Christian St.
White River Junction, VT 05001
www.nomadpress.net

Printed in the United States.

CONTENTS

PS

Interested in Primary Sources?

Look for this icon. Use a smartphone or tablet app to scan the QR code and explore more! You can find a list of URLs on the Resources page. If the QR code doesn't work, try searching the Internet with the Keyword Prompts to find other helpful sources.

 extinction 🔍

GEOLOGIC TIME SCALE

era: a division of geologic time.

period: a division of time within an era.

epoch: a division of time within a period.

WORDS TO KNOW

The timeline of Earth's lifespan is shown in a geologic time scale. It is broken up into chunks of time called **eras**. Each era is made up of different **periods**. Some of the more recent periods are also divided into **epochs**.

MILLIONS OF YEARS AGO

4,600		541.0	485.4	443.4	419.2	358.9	323.2

Paleozoic

Precambrian | Cambrian | Ordovician | Silurian | Devonian | Mississippian | Pennsylvanian

Age of Marine Invertebrates | | **Age of Fishes** | | **Age of Amphibians**

Origin of life

Early bacteria and algae

Simple multicelled organisms

Complex multicelled organisms

Early shelled organisms

Rise of corals

Trilobite maximum

Primitive fish

First land plants

First forests (evergreens)

First amphibians

Sharks abundant

First reptiles

Coal-forming swamps

MASS EXTINCTION

MASS EXTINCTION

FORMATION OF EARTH

iv

This geologic time scale includes important events in Earth's history. Some of these events include the appearance and disappearance of different species, major changes in the earth that have caused mass extinctions, and how the planet has changed.

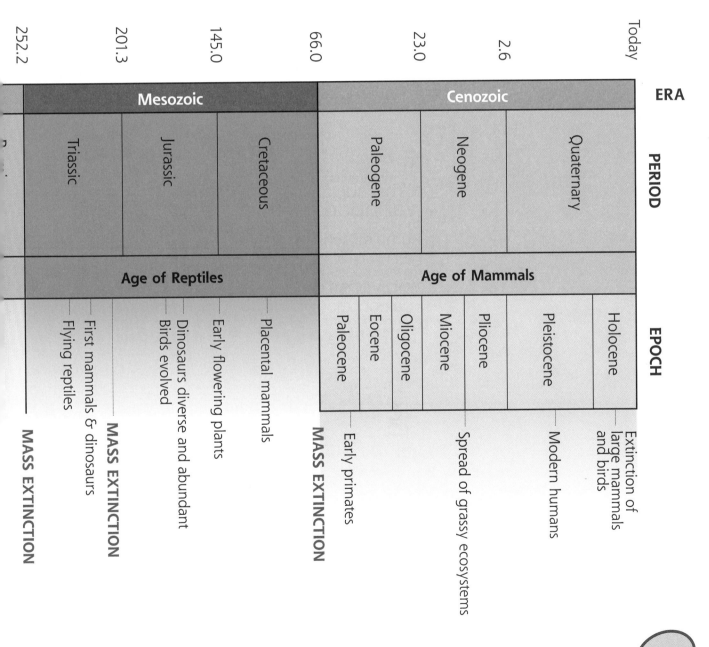

	Mesozoic			Cenozoic			ERA
252.2	Triassic (201.3)	Jurassic (145.0)	Cretaceous (66.0)	Paleogene (23.0)	Neogene (2.6)	Quaternary (Today)	PERIOD
	Age of Reptiles			Age of Mammals			
	Flying reptiles / First mammals & dinosaurs	Birds evolved / Dinosaurs diverse and abundant	Early flowering plants / Placental mammals	Paleocene / Eocene / Oligocene (Early primates)	Miocene / Pliocene (Spread of grassy ecosystems)	Pleistocene (Modern humans) / Holocene (Extinction of large mammals and birds)	EPOCH
MASS EXTINCTION	MASS EXTINCTION		MASS EXTINCTION				

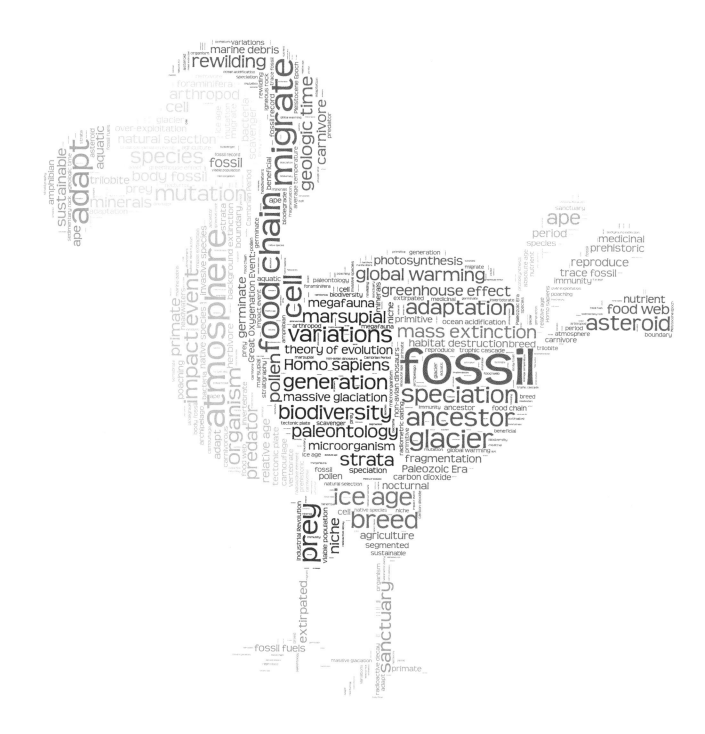

WHAT IS EXTINCTION?

You've probably heard the word **"extinction"** before. What does it make you think of? For many people, when they think about extinction, they think about dinosaurs. But dinosaurs represent only a very small percent of species that have gone extinct in the history of life on Earth. In fact, more than 5 billion species have gone extinct! That's more than 99 percent of all species that have ever lived on Earth.

Extinction occurs when the very last member of a species dies. It's rare that humans are able to observe this happening in real time. One opportunity came with a tortoise called Lonesome George. George was a Pinta Island tortoise. He was very old when he died. No one knows for sure, but they guessed that he was more than 100 years old. He had a broad, curved back, stubby legs, and a long, thin, wrinkled neck.

WORDS TO KNOW

extinction: when the last living member of a species dies.

species: a group of plants or animals that are closely related and produce offspring.

1

prehistoric: long ago, before written history.

ancestor: someone from your family who lived before you.

archipelago: a group of islands.

breed: to produce offspring.

WORDS TO KNOW

George's face was also wrinkled, and drawn tight over his mouth. He looked like the character Yoda from *Star Wars*, wise and **prehistoric**. At the end of his life, George was very well taken care of. He lived in a nice place where he was closely watched and doted on. He had lots of visitors.

When George died on June 24, 2012, the news made headlines around the world. People everywhere mourned his death, even though most had never met him. The world watched a species go extinct right before its eyes.

George's story actually began hundreds of years ago, when humans first started sailing the seas. Pinta Island tortoises lived on a tiny island in the Pacific that was part of a group of islands called the Galápagos Islands.

Because of the location of the islands, they were extremely important to early sailors. It was the perfect place for pirates, whalers, fishermen, and other sailors to stock up on fresh food. The tortoises were a source of fresh meat needed for long voyages.

DID YOU KNOW? Outside of Lonesome George's enclosure, there was a sign for visitors to read: "Whatever happens to this single animal, let him always remind us that the fate of all living things on Earth is in human hands."

Sailors first came upon the Galápagos Islands in the 1500s. At the time, many species of tortoises were plentiful. And to hungry humans, each tortoise represented hundreds of pounds of protein. This was bad news for the tortoises, especially because their giant size and overall slowness made them so easy to catch. Tens of thousands were captured and killed and eaten.

By the early 1900s, many turtle populations had been wiped out.

In fact, the Pinta Island tortoise was thought to be extinct by then. That is, until a single individual was found wandering around alone in the early 1970s. Like many of his **ancestors**, George was loaded onto a ship. But he wasn't killed. He was handled very carefully. George was taken to a tortoise center on Santa Cruz Island, another one of the 19 islands in the Galápagos **archipelago**.

Soon after his arrival, the tortoise was given the name Lonesome George. He was the last known Pinta Island tortoise. Scientists looked all around the world for a female tortoise to become George's mate. The hope was that if they could **breed**, the species could be saved. But a good mate was never found. George was known as the rarest creature on Earth. When he died in 2012, the Pinta Island tortoise was officially extinct. George's life and death became a symbol for all species facing extinction.

DEFINING EXTINCTION

In George's case, he was the last Pinta Island tortoise on Earth, and his death marked the extinction of that species. Scientists become concerned about a species going extinct when individuals in a species die at a faster rate than they are born.

PS

News of George

When Lonesome George died, people all around the world took notice. You can read an article about his life and death at this website. Why did his death have such an impact on so many people? Do you think humans learned any lessons from George?

Lonesome George NYT 🔎

WORDS TO KNOW

viable population: a group with enough individuals to breed and produce offspring so they can maintain their numbers and survive in the wild.

conservation: managing and protecting natural resources.

endangered: a plant or animal species with a dangerously low population.

reptile: an animal covered with scales that crawls on its belly or on short legs. Snakes, turtles, and alligators are reptiles.

mammal: a type of animal, such as a human, dog, or cat. Mammals are usually born live, feed milk to their young, and usually have hair or fur covering most of their skin.

organism: any living thing.

bacteria: tiny organisms found in animals, plants, soil, and water.

fossil: the remains or traces of ancient plants or animals left in rock.

When the number of individuals falls below a certain level, scientists consider whether there are enough of a species left to maintain a **viable population**. If the numbers fall too low, the species becomes "threatened with extinction." That means the species is in real trouble.

The International Union for the **Conservation** of Nature (IUCN) figures out which animals are at risk. The biologists there have created a list to keep track of **endangered** species. The IUCN Red List has three categories for animals in danger of becoming extinct: vulnerable, endangered, and critically endangered.

When we talk about extinction, we are not referring just to **reptiles** such as tortoises and **mammals** such as dinosaurs. All types of **organisms**, including plants, fungi, and **bacteria**, can go extinct.

One example is a group of trees known as *Lepidodendron* or "scale trees." They lived in hot, humid swamps more than 300 million years ago.

Lepidodendron were once as common as pine and oak trees are today. They were huge, growing to be 180 feet tall with trunks that could be 6 feet wide. The leaves of scale trees were like thick blades of grass clustered together. By the end of the Mesozoic era, 65 million years ago, this type of tree had gone extinct.

HISTORY OF EXTINCTION

For a long time, humans didn't consider that a species could go extinct. They didn't even think about whether or not animals or plants had a history. Even when strange **fossils** were found, people thought they must be the remains of living species. This changed during the eighteenth century, thanks to a tooth and a man named Georges Cuvier (1769–1832).

The tooth was found in the 1700s, in what is now the United States, near the Ohio River. French soldiers were camped along the river where Kentucky is today. Nearby, there was a marshy area that contained hundreds of very large bones. One thigh bone, a femur, was 3½ feet long. The men also found a tusk and many very large teeth.

Despite the difficulties of the trip, the troops were ordered to take the bones with them. The strange bones were lugged all the way to New Orleans, Louisiana, and then shipped to France and examined. People first thought they were some sort of elephant bones because elephants were a familiar species.

climate change: a change in the long-term average weather patterns of a place.

habitat: the natural area where a plant or animal lives.

herbivore: an animal that eats only plants.

WORDS TO KNOW

But the bones puzzled others who studied them. They agreed that the femur and tusks could be from an elephant, but the tooth was different from any other elephant tooth.

Elephants have flat teeth, which provide a good surface for chewing plants. However, the tooth that the French soldiers had found was cusped. The edges of the found tooth were pointed, much like a human molar—except that the molar the soldiers had found had roots the size of a human hand!

A debate began. Some people thought the bones belonged to two different animals. They suggested that the femur and tusk belonged to an elephant, and the tooth to a hippopotamus. Other people argued that the bones found in the New World were from three animals: an elephant, a hippopotamus, and some unknown species. Another scientist suggested that the bones all belonged to what he called an "American elephant."

Even President Thomas Jefferson (1743–1826) weighed in on the debate. He believed that the creature was still on the North American continent somewhere. He hoped that when Meriwether Lewis and William Clark set out on their expedition to explore the New World in 1804, that they would come across the unknown creature. As you can probably guess, they did not find the massive beast during their explorations.

DID YOU KNOW?

Even bacteria can be fossilized! The oldest bacteria fossils are thought to be almost 3.5 billion years old. The fossilized bacteria are very similar to bacteria alive today.

Mastodons

Many people confuse mastodons with woolly mammoths. While they do have some similarities, they are, in fact, different species. The beast that was found near the Ohio River in the late 1700s was eventually named the American mastodon. These giant creatures roamed North and Central America until about 10,000 years ago. Scientists are not sure why the mastodon went extinct. Some believe that humans, who lived there at the same time, were responsible. Recent studies suggest that **climate change**, changes in the creatures' **habitats**, disease, or some combination of these may have been the cause.

Based on fossils collected, scientists figured out that grown mastodons were between 7 and 14 feet tall. Full-grown adult male mastodons could weigh as much as 6 tons. They were also covered in fur, which protected them from harsh weather. The teeth of mastodons, such as the one found by the French soldiers, show that the mastodons were **herbivores**. The cusps on their teeth, which are not present on elephant or mammoth teeth, allowed them to crush twigs and branches. The mastodons had flexible trunks like elephants, and long, curved tusks. Remains of the American mastodon have been found all over the United States and down into South America.

In the late 1700s, a young man named Georges Cuvier began to study the strange bones from the New World. He compared the molar found near the Ohio River to elephants in Africa and Asia. After studying a lot of bones, Cuvier decided that the beast from North America was a different species entirely and no longer existed.

WORDS TO KNOW

paleontology: the study of the history of life on Earth. A paleontologist studies paleontology.

extirpated: to be completely missing from a certain area a species used to occupy.

sanctuary: a safe place.

carnivorous: describes a plant or animal that eats only animals.

native species: a species that naturally belongs in an ecosystem.

ecosystem: a community of living and nonliving things and their **environment**. Living things are plants, animals, and insects. Nonliving things are soil, rocks, and water.

environment: everything in nature, living and nonliving, including plants, animals, soil, rocks, and water.

As he continued his work, Cuvier came across other "lost species." He concluded that if several extinct species had been discovered, there might be many more. Because of his work, Cuvier is often thought of as the father of **paleontology**. At the time, the idea that a species could completely die out was new to scientists. But the more Cuvier studied bones and fossils, the more lost species he discovered. Soon, the idea of extinction became widely accepted by scientists.

OTHER TYPES OF EXTINCTION

Usually when we think of extinction, we think a species has died out completely. But a species can be considered extinct in an area. The scientific word for that is **extirpated**.

One example is the Canadian lynx. Hundreds of years ago, the lynx lived in the Rocky Mountains from southern Colorado into Canada. But when European settlers began to move across the continent in the 1800s, lynx numbers in the southern Rockies fell.

The settlers trapped the lynx for their furs. They also trapped and poisoned them because the lynx were seen as a threat. Much of the lynx habitat was destroyed as the country developed. The last known lynx in Colorado was killed in the early 1970s. While lynx still lived in the northern part of the Rockies, they were extirpated from Colorado. In the 1990s and into the 2000s, Colorado Parks and Wildlife worked to bring the lynx back to the state.

Species can also be declared "extinct in the wild." This means that no living members of a species live in the wild.

These species are not completely extinct, though. They can still exist in zoos, **sanctuaries**, and other places in captivity. In many cases, the species are kept in captivity to keep them from disappearing from Earth.

The Polynesian tree snail can no longer be found in the wild. However, prior to the species going extinct, snails were collected by researchers in the late 1970s. Now, the snails are part of an international breeding program. Conservation programs such as this help keep some species safe from extinction, even though most of the individuals will never live in the wild again.

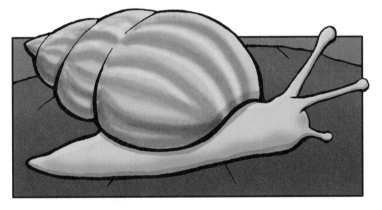

In the case of the tree snail, there may be hope. The snail first became threatened when another, **carnivorous** snail was introduced on the Polynesian islands. The non-native snail wiped out the **native species** of snails in the **ecosystem**.

Today, biologists are trying to control the carnivorous snail. They hope to reintroduce the Polynesian tree snail back into the wild. If they do this, the tree snail will be closely monitored.

In this book, you'll learn about the different causes of extinction and the histories of the major extinctions that have happened on Earth. We'll also look at some of the ways people are trying to prevent extinction, and what that means for the planet.

Good Science Practices

Every good scientist keeps a science journal! Scientists use the scientific method to keep their experiments organized. The scientific method is the way scientists ask questions and do experiments to try to prove their ideas. Choose a notebook to use as your science journal. As you read through this book and do the activities, keep track of your observations and record each step in a scientific method worksheet, like the one shown here.

Question: What are we trying to find out? What problem are we trying to solve?
Research: What information is already known about the topic?
Hypothesis/Prediction: What do we think the answer will be?
Equipment: What supplies are we using?
Method: What procedure are we following?
Results: What happened? Why?

Each chapter of this book begins with an essential question to help guide your exploration of extinction. Keep the question in your mind as you read the chapter. At the end of each chapter, use your science journal to record your thoughts and answers.

? ESSENTIAL QUESTION

Should humans try to prevent extinction from happening to existing species? Why or why not?

Kitchen Paleontologist

IDEAS FOR SUPPLIES

3–4 cups of rice, quinoa, or oatmeal
🌀 *3–4 kinds of pretzels of different sizes and shapes*

When paleontologists discover fossil bones, they are usually scattered across an area. Sometimes, the bones of more than one creature are mixed together. Perhaps the bones can be put together, but a piece is missing. This activity will give you an idea of what paleontologists do.

Spread the rice out into a wide, shallow dish. Break each pretzel into three to five pieces and mix them into the rice. It may be more fun, and more of a challenge, if you have someone do this step for you!

Dig the pieces back out and try to fit them together just as scientists fit together fossils to recreate the entire skeleton.

✱ What tools can you use to help yourself build the entire pretzel?

✱ Were you able to find all the pretzel bones during your first dig? If not, what did you do?

✱ Were you able to put a whole pretzel back together? Were there pieces missing?

✱ What steps do you think a paleontologist might take in the field to collect bones and keep them safe?

DID YOU KNOW?

In 1877, a paleontologist named Othniel Charles Marsh (1831–1899) accidently put the wrong skull on an *Apatosaurus*'s skeleton, creating a whole new breed of dinosaur that never actually existed—the *Brontosaurus*!

CONSIDER THIS: Why is it important to keep an open mind while assembling the parts of a whole? What dangers might paleontologists face when they make assumptions about what a skeleton is supposed to look like?

ACTIVITY

11

Canine Skeletal System

For this project, you will need the template at NomadPress.net/Templates

Georges Cuvier spent a lot of time studying the bones of animals. By looking closely at these bones, he was able to learn a lot about what the animal was like when it was alive. Can you piece together the bones on the template and discover what kind of animal they belong to?

Note: When you are finished, check the answer in the resources section.

First, look at the different bones. What can you tell about the animal by looking at its teeth? What do you notice about its feet? Do you think this animal walked on two legs or four? Before putting the skeleton together, can you predict what kind of animal this might be?

Cut out the different bones and put them together. When you are happy with your skeleton, secure it with tape.

Once you put the skeleton together, sketch out a body around it. Parts such as ears, skin, and fur would not be fossilized. Make a guess about these parts of the animal and what they looked like.

Assume that an inch equals a foot. How big do you think this animal was when it was alive?

CONSIDER THIS: What kind of animal do these bones belong to? Think about animals you are familiar with that have the same kind of teeth and feet. Also think about animals that would be about the same size. Would this project have been more difficult if some of the bones were missing?

Chapter 1

THE CAUSES OF EXTINCTION

The history of the earth is like an action adventure movie. Some parts of the story are thrilling. Some parts are violent. There are also parts that are sad, magical, and uplifting. Much of the earth's story is a mystery. There is much we don't know simply because we weren't there. The only recordkeepers were the rocks, and even studying the rocks can't answer all of our questions.

We want to know what kinds of life were on Earth millions of years ago. Also, what causes species to go extinct? In its whole history, Earth has been home to billions of different species of plants, animals, reptiles, bacteria, and other organisms. And 99 percent of those species have gone extinct. That's a lot! How does this happen?

? **ESSENTIAL QUESTION**

What causes a species to go extinct?

geologic time: the span of Earth's history marked by major events and changes.

gravity: the force that pulls objects toward each other and holds you on Earth.

lava: hot, melted rock that has risen to Earth's surface.

cell: the basic building block for all life on Earth.

microorganism: a living thing that is so small it can only be seen with a microscope.

photosynthesis: the process a plant goes through to make its own food. The plant uses water and carbon dioxide in the presence of sunlight to make oxygen and sugar.

atmosphere: the mixture of gases surrounding Earth.

cyanobacteria: a type of aquatic bacteria that produces oxygen through photosynthesis.

Great Oxygenation Event: the introduction of oxygen into Earth's atmosphere more than 2 billion years ago.

A BRIEF HISTORY OF LIFE ON EARTH

To understand the story of the earth, we must start at the beginning of **geologic time**. Planet Earth took shape about 4.5 billion years ago.

The planet formed from a massive cloud of dust, rocks, and gas swirling through space.

As time passed, **gravity** gathered these particles together. More objects joined the mass. It grew larger and larger.

Have you ever made a snowball? The building blocks of a snowball are the tiny flakes. You are the gravity pushing the flakes together. To make the snowball bigger, you add another handful of snow. Then another. Soon you have the perfect snowball. Or, in the case of Earth, a perfect planet. Except back then, it was very, very hot—more than 2,000 degrees Fahrenheit (1,094 degrees Celsius)! There was no oxygen. And no water. The surface of Earth looked like a sea of bubbling **lava**.

As Earth cooled, a crust formed on top, providing solid land. And then, about 3.5 billion years ago, life on Earth began. The first life forms were very simple. They were very small organisms made of just one **cell**.

2,000°F
(1,094°C)

Scientists still don't know much about these single-celled **microorganisms**. However, research has shown that these early life forms were the ancestors of bacteria we have today!

For millions of years, these organisms used the sun's energy for **photosynthesis**. They released oxygen, which slowly built up in the earth's **atmosphere**. Eventually, there was enough oxygen in the air to sustain organisms that did not rely on the sun for energy. Scientists do not understand the details of how this happened, but they do credit an organism called **cyanobacteria** for playing a major role in this step, called the **Great Oxygenation Event**.

DID YOU KNOW?

Have you read the story "Goldilocks and the Three Bears?" Earth is called a "Goldilocks planet." It is not too far from the sun. It is not too close to the sun. It is just the right distance away to support life.

evolve: to gradually develop through time.

invertebrate: an animal that does not have a backbone. A vertebrate is an animal with a backbone.

Cambrian Period: the first period of the Paleozoic Era, marked by an explosion of life.

trilobite: an ancient arthropod that lived during the Paleozoic Era.

marine: of or relating to the ocean.

arthropod: an invertebrate animal with a segmented body and limbs with joints, such as a spider or insect.

segmented: divided into parts.

exoskeleton: a hard shell or cover on the outside of an organism that provides support and protection.

predator: an animal that hunts another animal for food.

amphibian: a cold-blooded animal, such as a toad, frog, or salamander, that needs sunlight to keep warm and shade to stay cool. Amphibians live on land and in the water.

Simple, multi-celled organisms **evolved** first. Then, about 600 million years ago, complex multi-celled organisms evolved. This was the beginning of simple plants and animals. These simple animals included **invertebrates**, such as jellyfish, worms, and sea sponges.

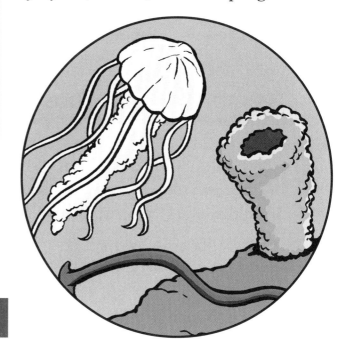

An explosion of life on Earth during the Cambrian Period occurred between 543 and 490 million years ago.

From then on, life on Earth changed very quickly. It also became more diverse. **Trilobites** evolved, then clams, snails, and corals. Later came fish. Up to this point, the only life on Earth was in the oceans. The first land plants evolved about 440 million years ago. Once there was plant life on land, animal species moved out of the water.

PS SPECIES SPOTLIGHT

Trilobites

Trilobites look like a mash-up of a scorpion, a horseshoe crab, and a turtle! You won't find one in today's oceans. Trilobites have been extinct for about 250 million years. Before that, during the Paleozoic Era, they lived on the ocean floor. Trilobites ranged in size from less than half an inch to more than 2 feet long. They were **marine arthropods**, a type of invertebrate similar to many of today's insects, spiders, and crustaceans. They had a **segmented** body and limbs with joints. The trilobites also had an **exoskeleton**. This hard, outer shell protected them. That might have been part of the reason they survived for 250 to 300 million years!

One of the interesting things about trilobites was their eyes. Each one had hundreds of parts, similar to the eyes of today's flies. Trilobites could see almost 360 degrees around. This came in handy when they were trying to spot **predators**!

A trilobite fossil

The first land creatures were insects. Then came **amphibians**, reptiles, and dinosaurs. About 220 million years ago, the first mammals evolved. These are the species that start to look a little more like the animals we have today. Only 200,000 years ago, humans emerged. Since then, humans have moved across all the continents on Earth. We made tools that helped us hunt, built shelters, made fire, and developed transportation.

WORDS TO KNOW

speciation: the evolution of a new species.

mutation: a permanent change in DNA.

DNA: deoxyribonucleic acid. The substance found in your cells that carries your genes, the genetic information that contains the "blueprint" of who you are.

evolution: the **theory** of how species develop from earlier forms of life, through natural **variations**.

theory: an idea that tries to explain why something is the way it is.

variations: the differences among members of a species.

beneficial: having good or helpful results.

generation: a group born and living at about the same time.

reproduce: to make something new, just like itself. To have babies.

background extinction: the ongoing, normal process of species going extinct.

SPECIATION

How did new species that could live on land evolve? The process, called **speciation**, begins with **mutations** in **DNA**. Your DNA is like your body's code for how to develop. You can think of DNA as a recipe that your body follows to make you who you are.

For evolution to happen, the DNA of a creature needs to change just enough to affect something about a species.

Perhaps the change causes an animal's fur to be a little different. If that fur color happens to better protect the animal from predators, that animal will live longer and produce more babies. Those babies might inherit the mutation for better fur color.

During long periods of time, this **beneficial** mutation can spread through the entire population. Sometimes, mutations cause individuals in a population to become so different from those of other populations of the same species that they can't produce offspring with each other. From that point onward, biologists consider the two populations to be two different species.

SPECIES SPOTLIGHT

Shark!

The first sharks appeared about 420 million years ago. Some of them were very strange looking, while others looked like the sharks we see today. Learn more about the evolution of sharks and get to know some of the prehistoric species in this video. Why do you think sharks have been able to survive for millions of years? What do you think they might be like in another few million years?

Interactive shark evolution timeline 🔍

One thing to remember is that evolution takes place during millions and millions of years. It's not as though a fish woke up one day and decided to take a walk on the beach! Instead, the changes happened bit by bit, not to individual organisms but to the species as a whole. Each **generation** of plants or animals produced offspring that were slightly different from them, and future offspring were a little more different, and so on. This happened until the offspring were so different from the original organisms that they could be classified as a new species. We will talk about that in more detail in Chapter 5.

BACKGROUND EXTINCTIONS

During all those billions of years that life on Earth was evolving, most species didn't last. Species evolve, **reproduce**, thrive, then decline. Eventually, they go extinct. This natural process is called **background extinction**. It happens very gradually and extinction comes slowly. But why? What causes a species to die off?

DID YOU KNOW? Today, there are more than 7 billion people on Earth. In 1800, there were only 1 billion. By the year 2050, scientists predict there will be 9.7 billion people on the planet.

The simple reason a species goes extinct is that it doesn't **adapt** to changes in its environment. Sometimes, the changes in a species' habitat are too great. Habitat changes can occur because of changes in temperature or precipitation. Environmental changes can even cause a loss of habitat for a species.

Other species go extinct because they can't compete with a new species that evolves. Disease can also wipe out a species. Sometimes, one species goes extinct because another species they rely on as a food source goes extinct.

Entire food chains can collapse if species don't adapt to changes.

Many of the environmental changes happening today are caused by human activity. In addition, today's rate of extinction is much greater than the normal background extinction rate. This has scientists worried. We will talk about this in detail in Chapter 6.

MASS EXTINCTIONS

There is another type of extinction you might already be familiar with. It is called **mass extinction**. This is the type of extinction that happened when most groups of dinosaurs went extinct. These dinosaurs didn't gradually die off because of background extinctions. Instead, they disappeared very quickly. Of course, quickly in geologic time still means hundreds or thousands of years!

Around the same time many dinosaur groups went extinct, many other species also went extinct. Mass extinctions are the result of one event that wipes out more than 50 percent of all species on Earth. There have been at least five mass extinctions in Earth's history.

DID YOU KNOW?

We often refer to dinosaurs as being extinct, but it was **non-avian dinosaurs** that died out. Birds, which are a species of dinosaur, are still around!

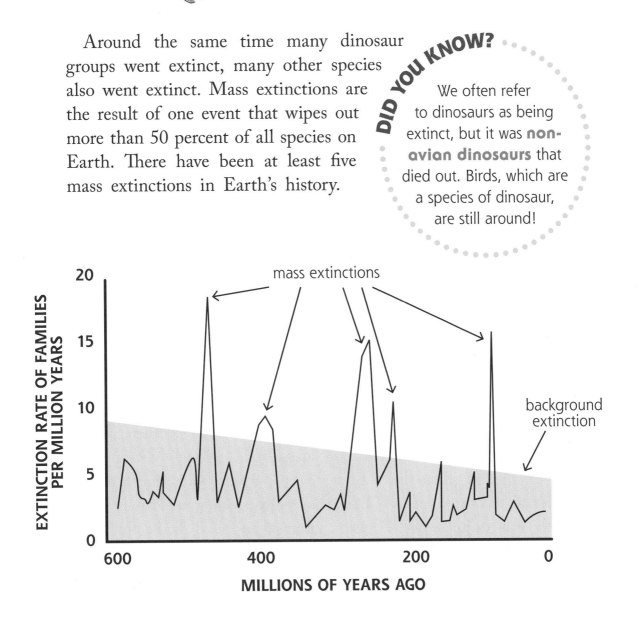

Scientists have a pretty good understanding of the causes of background extinction. But mass extinctions are more difficult to explain. They are like unsolved mysteries. So far, scientists know that these events happened. They also know when they happened. While they don't know what caused most mass extinctions, they do have some ideas.

carbon dioxide: a colorless, odorless gas. It forms when animals breathe and when plants and other living matter die and rot.

asteroid: a small, rocky object orbiting the sun. Asteroids are too small to be planets.

impact event: when objects from outer space hit Earth.

pollen: a fine, yellow powder produced by flowering plants. Pollen fertilizes the seeds of other plants as it gets spread around by the wind, birds, and insects.

debris: the pieces left after something has been destroyed.

Paleozoic Era: a period of time in Earth's history, between 541 and 252 million years ago, when complex forms of life evolved.

One possible explanation for a mass extinction is a significant rise in the amount of **carbon dioxide** in the atmosphere. The release of too much of this gas would make it hard for many species to survive. Massive volcanic eruptions are another suspect in mass extinction mysteries. These are eruptions that were so large, the dust and ash covered entire continents. Plus, they released huge amounts of gases into the atmosphere.

Climate change, either from hot to cold or cold to hot, is another suspect in the case of mass extinctions. Throughout Earth's history, there have been many periods when most of the planet was covered in ice. There have also been many times when Earth was quite warm. These changes can be difficult for some species to adapt to. It's also possible that a combination of circumstances can cause a mass extinction.

Not all mass extinctions have been a result of changes that originated on Earth. **Asteroids** from space are also on the list of suspects. When the planet is hit by a massive asteroid, it is called an **impact event**. These events kill everything in the direct path of the asteroid.

PS

Pollen Fossils

When we think about fossils, we often think of dinosaur bones or impressions of leaves in a rock. Did you ever think about paleontologists looking at the fossils of **pollen**? It turns out that grains of pollen make great fossils. Not only are there a lot of them, but they are very hardy.

Paleontologists use a special process to remove pollen fossils from the rocks. From the samples, scientists can figure out what types of plants and animals lived during certain time periods. These samples also offer clues about the climate. Paleontologists can get so much information from one small sample that they can reconstruct prehistoric landscapes. You can see photographs of pollen fossils here.

fossil park pollen 🔍

The impact of an asteroid releases dust and **debris** into Earth's atmosphere. This can lead to great changes in the climate and environment.

The most interesting thing about the mass extinctions in the past is that some species did survive. Many species were completely wiped out and the earth's environment changed drastically, but other species had the opportunity to thrive.

The three main eras of life on Earth we will focus on in this book are the Paleozoic, the Mesozoic, and the Cenozoic. Before those eras, in the Precambrian time, life on Earth was very, very simple. Yet, beginning in the Cambrian Period of the **Paleozoic Era**, that began to change.

? ESSENTIAL QUESTION

Now it's time to consider and discuss the Essential Question:
What causes a species to go extinct?

Geologic Timeline

Create your own geologic timeline to help you to understand Earth's history. We are used to thinking in terms of decades and centuries, but when you think about the history of Earth, you need to think in terms of millions and billions of years!

Draw a timeline the length of your paper (a very long piece of paper works best!). Mark one end of the timeline "4.5 billion years ago." That's when Earth formed. Mark the other end "today."

Now it's time for a little math. Using a calculator, figure out how many inches on your timeline equals 100 million years. Another way to do it would be to divide the timeline in half. That halfway point would be 2,250 million years ago. Then divide it again. And again, and again. This is the part where you might want to ask for help! Mark dates on the timeline by how many million years ago they were.

DID YOU KNOW?

Between 66 and 34 million years ago, Earth was much warmer than it is today. There were no polar ice caps, and palm trees and crocodiles thrived in the Arctic!

Once you have dates on the timeline, use your pencil to mark important times in Earth's history. You can use the dates provided in the geologic time scale in the front of this book. With an adult's permission, you can also do your own research on the Internet.

* When did certain species evolve?   * When did humans evolve?
* When did the first reptiles emerge?

CONSIDER THIS: Look at your finished timeline. What do you notice? Does it look like you expected it to look? Think about how long humans have been on Earth compared to Earth's whole history.

Thank You, Phytoplankton!

Even if you don't live anywhere near an ocean, you still have phytoplankton to thank for the oxygen in our atmosphere. Phytoplankton are microscopic marine plants, usually single-celled, that drift on the currents of the oceans. These microscopic organisms produce about half of the oxygen on Earth. The other half is produced by land plants and trees. So, hug a tree and thank a phytoplankton! With this experiment, you can figure out just how important phytoplankton are.

Create a chart in your science journal to keep track of the number of breaths you take in 30-second chunks of time.

Sit down and get comfortable. Have a timer handy or have a friend or parent use the timer. Count the number of breaths you take in 30 seconds. Record the number in your chart.

Now calculate how many breaths you take in 1 minute (multiply the number of breaths in 30 seconds by two). If you took nine breaths in 30 seconds, your answer would be 18 breaths in a minute. Record the number in your science journal.

Do the math to figure out how many breaths you take in an hour and in day. When you have the number of breaths you take in a day, divide by two. You now know how many of your breaths in a day are thanks to phytoplankton!

CONSIDER THIS: What would happen if phytoplankton numbers started to decrease? Why is it important to protect their environment, the ocean? Can you think of ways to decrease the amount of pollution in oceans?

Chapter 2

THE PALEOZOIC ERA

The first period of the Paleozoic Era is the Cambrian Period. After 3 billion years of life on Earth, this was when life on Earth really **diversified**. In the oceans, shelled creatures, coral, and fish evolved. For the first time, these creatures had heads, fins or legs, and eyes.

About 100 million years later, the first land plants evolved. Then came insects and, later, amphibians. Eventually, reptiles emerged. Toward the end of the Paleozoic Era, the evolution of the very first mammal-like creatures set the stage for all later mammals that came during the Mesozoic Era.

The Paleozoic Era lasted about 300 million years. It is divided into seven different time periods. Look back at the geologic time scale in the front of this book. At the same time that life was evolving and becoming more diverse, there were three mass extinction events, called the End Ordovician Extinction, Late Devonian Extinction, and the Permian Extinction.

? ESSENTIAL QUESTION

What might life be like on Earth today if the Great Dying hadn't happened?

This third event wiped out almost everything. How did the "Great Dying" happen?

THE END ORDOVICIAN EXTINCTION

Imagine that you are a lead investigator on a case. Pets in the neighborhood have gone missing. Your job is to figure out what happened to them. Where do you start your investigation? Interviewing witnesses? Good idea! But what happens if the witnesses are no longer available? Now what do you do?

Maybe you try to put together a timeline of what you do know. Maybe you look for clues. This type of detective work is exactly what paleontologists do to try to understand the history of life on Earth, including extinction. Sometimes, scientists can solve the case this way. But other times, they can't.

The planet must be in balance for life to thrive.

Temperature affects that balance. It needs to stay within a certain range. On Earth, temperature is partly regulated by carbon dioxide in the atmosphere. One of the things carbon dioxide does is trap heat in our atmosphere. Therefore, the more carbon dioxide, the warmer the temperatures. The opposite is also true. If the amount of carbon dioxide lessens, the temperature drops. Temperature depends on other factors as well, such as the distance the planet is from the sun.

What happens if the temperature falls too much? Everything freezes. That is exactly what happened at the end of the Ordovician Period.

DID YOU KNOW?

The U.S. National Parks are home to many fossils and rocks that have helped scientists and **geologists** learn more about the history of Earth.

glacier: a semi-permanent mass of ice that moves very, very slowly down a mountain or slope.

massive glaciation: the widespread formation of sheets of ice.

erosion: when land is worn away by wind or water.

foraminifera: single-celled marine organisms with shells, also called forams.

minerals: a naturally occurring solid found in rocks and in the ground. Rocks are made of minerals. Gold and diamonds are precious minerals.

sedimentary rock: rock that is formed by deposits of sediment that settle to the bottom of water and are hardened from pressure.

fossil record: the total number of fossils found in the rock layers.

WORDS TO KNOW

About 444 million years ago, temperatures on Earth dropped. Oceans froze. Sea levels lowered. Glaciers formed over much of Earth. Many species lost their habitats. Others lost food sources. And, likely, many simply couldn't adapt to the temperature change. Some scientists maintain that as much as 85 percent of species were wiped out. It may have been the second largest extinction event in Earth's history.

Massive glaciation is one possible reason for the End Ordovician Extinction. Why did it happen? What caused carbon dioxide levels to drop? Scientists don't know. One theory is that the early land plants were to blame.

How could tiny plants cause a mass extinction? There might have been so many plants pulling carbon dioxide out of the air that they caused temperatures to drop.

Another theory blames the uplift of the Appalachian Mountains and **erosion**. In this case, it is thought that as the rock eroded, the newly exposed rock absorbed carbon dioxide from the air.

PS

Foraminifera

Foraminifera, or forams for short, are single-celled marine organisms. They build a shell around themselves using **minerals** from the seawater. While they may be small, they are also mighty. The first forams appeared more than 500 million years ago, during the early part of the Paleozoic Era. Today, there are still 4,000 species of forams in the world's oceans! Forams past and present come in many different shapes and sizes. Most are very small, about 1 millimeter in size. The largest can be as big as 7.9 inches.

Foraminifera fossils are common in most marine **sedimentary rocks**. The forams in the **fossil record** have told scientists a lot about prehistoric life on Earth. Scientists study the chemical makeup of the forams' shells, which reveals information about the climate during different time periods in different places. It also tells scientists how the climate changed over time.

Not only are the forams very informative, they are fascinating to look at! Some have long, narrow, cone-shaped shells. Others are round with spikes. Some resemble snail shells we see today. You can see photos and a video of forams at these websites. What do the fossils look like to you?

Ocean Portal foraminifera 🔍

Smithsonian forams video 🔍

---

strata: layers of something.

stratigraphy: the study of the layers of rocks and their relation to geologic time.

relative age: the geologic age of rocks or fossils defined by location in the rock strata.

absolute age: a more precise age of rocks or fossils determined by radioactive decay.

radioactive element: a material that releases its energy and begins to decay.

igneous rock: rock that forms from cooling magma. Magma is melted rock below the surface of the earth.

radioactive decay: the process by which the small units that make up an object change and break down.

radiometric dating: a process that measures the decay of radioactive elements, used to determine the age of rocks and fossils.

WORDS TO KNOW

HOW DO SCIENTISTS KNOW WHAT THEY KNOW?

You might be wondering how scientists know as much as they do about time periods so long ago. They are good detectives! The information we know about the End Ordovician Extinction and others has come from studying rocks and fossils. There are no living witnesses to these events, but paleontologists know how to read the rocks.

Sedimentary rocks have layers called **strata**. Think of it like a layer cake. The layer on the bottom was set down first. Then maybe a layer of icing. Then another layer of cake. When the cake is cut, you can easily see the layers. You know which layer is the "oldest" just by looking at it.

When paleontologists study the strata, they learn the same things. This is called **stratigraphy**. Rocks and fossils near the surface are generally the youngest. And the farther down you go, the older the rocks and fossils.

Even though rocks around the world are all different types, they all have a story to tell.

You know exactly how old you are because you know when your birthday is. How do scientists figure out how old rocks and fossils are?

Can you see the different layers in the cliff? (U.S. Geological Survey)

Scientists must rely on the rocks and the fossils to reveal their ages. One way they do this is by determining **relative age**. Think again about the layer cake. If the rock layers are undisturbed, the strata of rocks near the surface are younger than the ones at the bottom. In this way, scientists can know that some rocks and fossils are older or younger than others, depending on what strata the fossils are found in.

With other techniques, scientists can also determine a more precise **absolute age**. In this case, scientists study the **radioactive elements** in the **igneous rocks** and minerals they find. These elements break down over time. Scientists know the rate of this **radioactive decay** for different elements.

When a rock is found, scientists measure the amount of certain elements. Based on the amount of radioactive decay, they know how old the rock is. This is called **radiometric dating**. Of course, it isn't as exact as knowing your birth date, and it only works for some rocks, but on the geologic time scale it is pretty accurate.

deduce: to make a logical conclusion based on evidence.

ice age: a period of time when ice covers a large part of Earth.

body fossil: a fossil that is formed from the hard parts of a animal or plant, such as bones, teeth, shells, or tree trunks.

trace fossil: a fossil that is formed from something other than a plant or animal's body, but that shows evidence of life, such as nests, egg shells, poop, burrows, footprints, or leaf impressions.

In the case of the End Ordovician Extinction, paleontologists looked at rocks that were about 444 million years old. They looked for fossils that were present below that layer. And they studied fossils that were present above that layer. Fossils below the layer showed them what kind of life lived on Earth during the Cambrian and Ordovician Periods. When they looked above that layer, they saw a sharp decrease in the number of fossils.

Scientists **deduced** that something must have happened to the species that were alive at the end of the Ordovician Period. When they looked for other clues, the rocks showed deposits from glaciers. That is why scientists think that an **ice age** was to blame for the extinction event.

Trace Fossils and Body Fossils

Fossils are evidence of prehistoric life. They are the silent witnesses buried in the rock that help scientists understand the mysteries of the past. These fossils come in two types: **body fossils** and **trace fossils**.

Body fossils are made from the actual bodies of prehistoric creatures or plants, including bones, skulls, teeth, and shells. The original bone is largely replaced with minerals. Trace fossils are fossils that were not part of the body, such as egg shells and even poop. These still provide evidence of past life. Trace fossils also include impressions left in the ground, such as dinosaur footprints or burrows made by worms. Imprints of ancient leaves are also trace fossils. Skin can leave impressions that become trace fossils. Both kinds of fossils are very important to scientists.

LATE DEVONIAN EXTINCTION

The End Ordovician Extinction led to a huge loss of life. However, this loss allowed other species to flourish. For the next 70 to 80 million years, life on Earth diversified.

The Devonian Period is known as the "age of fish." Sharks and amphibians emerged during this time and land plants began to diversify. About 360 million years ago, another mass extinction took place, known as the Late Devonian Extinction. Even though paleontologists know a lot about past life on Earth, they don't know much about this extinction event at all.

Scientists know it happened, but they aren't sure if it happened all at once or if there was more than one event separated by hundreds of thousands of years.

Whatever happened caused about 70 percent of species to go extinct. Just as with the end of the Ordovician Period, marine species were the most affected. Species that lived in shallow, warm seas were most impacted.

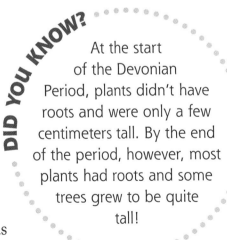

DID YOU KNOW? At the start of the Devonian Period, plants didn't have roots and were only a few centimeters tall. By the end of the period, however, most plants had roots and some trees grew to be quite tall!

nutrient: a substance in food and soil that living things need to live and grow.

algae: a simple organism found in water that is like a plant but without roots, stems, or leaves.

coniferous: describes cone-bearing shrubs and trees, often with needles for leaves. Coniferous trees do not lose their leaves each year.

warm-blooded: animals such as humans and bears that can keep themselves warm with their body heat.

boundary: in geology, the strata in the rock that marks the end of one period and the beginning of another.

biodiversity: many different species of plants and animals living in an area.

WORDS TO KNOW

There are a lot of theories about what caused the Late Devonian Extinction, including asteroids, climate change, and changes in sea level. Another theory suggests that the new plants on land were to blame. It was during the Devonian Period that land plants literally took root. Their roots grew deep into the ground, creating soil. These roots also broke down rocks, which released minerals and **nutrients**. All of this helped life on land thrive.

When these minerals and nutrients washed into the ocean, they provided a great food source for microscopic **algae**. The algae ate and ate and ate all of this food. Bacteria then broke down the algae. In the process of breaking down the algae, the bacteria used up all the oxygen. Maybe there wasn't enough oxygen in the water for fish to breathe. Unfortunately, paleontologists have been unable to locate clues that lead them closer to fully solving the mystery.

THE PERMIAN EXTINCTION: THE GREAT DYING

Life on Earth rebounded once again after the Late Devonian Extinction. By the end of the Paleozoic Era, during the Permian Period, there was a diversity of plants in freshwater and on land, including forests of **coniferous** trees. There was algae in the oceans. There were also both sea and land creatures.

The ocean was home to sharks and rays. On land, there were many insects, such as beetles, dragonflies, and cockroaches. Amphibians and reptiles roamed widely. There were also creatures that we have given strange names, such as *Lystrosaurus*, dicynodont, and gorgonopsian. Some of these were the ancestors of today's mammals. The skulls and jaws of these creatures were different from those of reptiles and more like today's mammals. In addition, their legs were under their bodies. Some were even thought to be **warm-blooded**.

This world was teeming with life when another mass extinction event occurred. The event resulted in what is called the Great Dying. It was the worst extinction event in Earth's history, wiping out about 90 percent of marine life and 75 percent of land animal species. Why? It is a 250-million-year-old murder mystery.

To solve this case, scientists once again turn to rocks. They look for the **boundary** in the rock layers between the Permian Period of the Paleozoic Era and the Triassic Period. Below the boundary is evidence of great **biodiversity** before the end of the Permian Period. Above the boundary, everything is different.

Which suspect was strong enough and quick enough to kill off so many species at one time?

One of the prime suspects is volcanic activity. Scientists aren't talking about just a single volcano. Instead, they are talking about a group of volcanoes erupting for long periods of time. In eastern Russia, there are remnants of volcanic activity called the Siberian Traps. This is where past volcanoes were thought to have spewed lava for a million years. This much lava would have covered an area as big as the United States. In some places, the lava was a mile deep.

ocean acidification: the process by which the ocean absorbs carbon dioxide from the atmosphere. Through a series of chemical reactions, the ocean becomes more acidic.

acidic: from acids, which are chemical compounds that taste sour, bitter, or tart. Examples are vinegar and lemon juice. Water also contains some acid.

WORDS TO KNOW

How could massive volcanoes in one part of the world affect the rest of the world? Think about dominoes. The small, flat tiles can be set up on end in a row, one after the other. If one tips over onto another, it knocks it down. Then the second domino knocks down the third, and so on, in a chain reaction.

This is exactly what scientists think happened when the volcanoes that produced the Siberian Traps erupted.

They spewed lava, which wiped out everything in its path. They also released gases, including a massive amount of carbon dioxide. The carbon dioxide trapped heat in the atmosphere, causing temperatures on Earth to rise and the oceans to warm. The chemistry of the ocean changed because warm water doesn't hold as much oxygen as cold water.

Flood Basalt Eruption

The volcanic activity that created the Siberian Traps was a flood basalt eruption. These eruptions are not just one, but many eruptions at a time. They also last for thousands or even millions of years. Flood basalt eruptions cover huge areas of land or the sea floor with basalt lava. These continuous eruptions occur as magma pushes through long cracks in Earth's crust.

In the northwestern United States, the Columbia Plateau formed as a result of a flood basalt eruption between 15 and 17 million years ago. It covers an area of more than 81,000 square miles, mostly in the states of Washington and Oregon.

Evidence suggests that **ocean acidification** also played a role in extinctions. When carbon dioxide is released into the atmosphere, much of it is absorbed by the ocean, making the ocean more **acidic**. Because of ocean acidification, many shelled marine species couldn't produce and maintain healthy shells. This included many reef-forming animals, such as corals and sponges. Other species of marine animals and plants, such as algae, might not have been able to tolerate water that was too acidic.

We don't know if scientists will ever be able to completely close the case of the Permian Extinction. We do know that they will continue to interview the suspects and look for clues.

? ESSENTIAL QUESTION

Now it's time to consider and discuss the Essential Question: What might life be like on Earth today if the Great Dying hadn't happened?

Make Your Own Fossil

IDEAS FOR SUPPLIES

plaster of Paris ☿ *organic materials, such as leaves, pinecones, and feathers*
☿ *disposable container, such as a paper cup*

Get a sense of how fossils are formed by creating your own!

Fill your container about halfway with the plaster. Press your **organic** material into the plaster. Let the first layer set for a few minutes. Then pour more plaster on top and let it harden.

Once the layers have hardened, cut away your container and begin your work as a paleontologist!

Separate your strata and find your fossils. What tools work best and do the least damage to your fossils? How do paleontologists ensure that they disturb the fossils as little as possible?

CONSIDER THIS: You may want to do the experiment again to perfect your fossils. Or try using other materials. Think about fossilization happening naturally. What makes the best fossils? Also consider the paleontologist's job. Are some fossils easier to find than others? Are some more difficult to remove than others? What happens if the fossils are clumped together?

WORDS TO KNOW

organic: of living things, or developing naturally.

ACTIVITY

Making Mountains

Mountains are formed in different ways. Fold mountains are formed when the earth's tectonic plates are pushed together. This activity will give you a sense of how fold mountains are formed. Take a look at how the different layers react when this type of mountain pushes upward.

Collect a bunch of bath towels of different colors. Five or more will work best. You'll also need two boxes, each about as wide as a folded towel. Fold all the towels in half and lay them on top of each other.

Put a box on either side of the towels. Before you push the boxes toward each other to squish the towels together, predict what you think will happen.

Now push the boxes toward each other. You've created fold mountains!

CONSIDER THIS: Was your hypothesis correct? What do you notice about the layers? If you do the experiment again, place "fossils" at each layer and see what happens. Now, imagine that wind and weather erode the top of the mountain. How might erosion affect what you see?

DID YOU KNOW?

Want to learn more about fossils? This virtual museum can help! It has photographs of fossils from all different geologic time periods. You can explore hundreds of photos and links to learn more about the fossil record across time.

WORDS TO KNOW

tectonic plate: a large section of the earth's crust that moves on top of the mantle, the layer beneath the crust.

virtual fossil museum 🔍

ACTIVITY

The Effect of Acidification on Shells

IDEAS FOR SUPPLIES

white vinegar ◉ jar ◉ egg

Sometimes, the ocean becomes acidic due to chemical changes in the atmosphere and the water. When this happens, shelled organisms have a hard time making shells. This experiment will investigate what happens to those organisms in an acidic ocean.

Put the egg in the jar and cover it with vinegar, which is an acidic liquid. What do you think will happen to the egg? Write your hypothesis in your science journal.

Let the egg sit in the jar for at least two days. Be careful getting the egg out!

* What happened to the shell?
* What does it feel like?
* What does it look like?
* Are the results what you predicted?
* What would happen to an ocean creature with a shell like that?

DID YOU KNOW?

At the end of the Ordovician Period, some **glacial deposits** were left in what is now the Sahara Desert! Of course, the area was not a desert then.

CONSIDER THIS: Try the experiment again with seashells. Predict what will happen to them. What happens if you let them sit in the vinegar for longer?

WORDS TO KNOW

glacial deposit: big rocks or stones left when a glacier moves or melts.

Chapter 3

THE MESOZOIC ERA

After the Great Dying of the Paleozoic Era, there was very little life on Earth. The air was difficult to breathe. The oceans were sick. Yet, very slowly, life came back. Life diversified and flourished once again.

Are you beginning to see a pattern? The Permian Extinction was the third mass extinction on Earth. It was the third time life had been nearly wiped out. It was also the third time life on Earth recovered. The End Permian Extinction marked the end of the Paleozoic Era and the beginning of the Mesozoic Era.

? ESSENTIAL QUESTION

What happened to the dinosaurs?

The Mesozoic era is divided into three periods—the Triassic, the Jurassic, and the Cretaceous. It is an era that is sometimes called the "Age of Dinosaurs" because dinosaurs roamed Earth for most of the Mesozoic Era—almost 100 million years.

Let's take a look at the two mass extinctions that occurred during the Mesozoic Era. These are the End Triassic Extinction and the End Cretaceous Extinction.

END TRIASSIC EXTINCTION

The Permian Extinction, like others before it, allowed new species to emerge. Life once again diversified. Reptiles and amphibians, such as snakes, crocodiles, salamanders, and frogs, thrived. The first flying reptiles appeared. And Earth's first mammals appeared. It was during the Triassic Period that dinosaurs evolved. These powerful creatures soon dominated Earth on land. In the ocean, giant sea reptiles such as the ichthyosaurus and the plesiosaurus ruled.

Coprolites

When scientists study prehistoric life, they investigate every clue. That includes ancient poop, called **coprolites**. Coprolites come in all sizes, including gigantic poops from dinosaurs. Because they are fossilized, they feel like rock. Paleontologists can't always tell what organism the coprolites are from. However, the coprolites do tell them about the diet of the organism. The coprolites are sliced open and examined under a microscope. This can reveal the remains of seeds, leaves, bones, teeth, and more. This also gives scientists clues about the organism's environment.

Then, about 200 million years ago, at the end of the Triassic Period, there was a fourth mass extinction.

The End Triassic Extinction is the one that scientists are most unsure about. Some think climate change was the culprit. Others have blamed volcanic eruptions. Still others think the extinction was the result of an asteroid strike. Whatever happened, about 80 percent of life on Earth was wiped out.

Think back to the first three extinctions you read about. What happened to life after the mass extinctions? The End Triassic Extinction was no different—many species died, but the mass extinction made room for other species to evolve. Life on Earth slowly recovered for millions of years. And, you guessed it, life continued to diversify.

Some dinosaurs survived the End Triassic Extinction. Once life rebounded during the Jurassic Period, those dinosaurs became more diverse. They evolved into much larger creatures, such as the *Stegosaurus*, the *Allosaurus*, the *Brachiosaurus*, and *Diplodocus*.

DID YOU KNOW?

The word *reptile* comes from a Latin word that means "creeping."

It was during this period that the feared *Tyrannosaurus rex* emerged. *Giganotosaurus*, *Triceratops*, and *Ankylosaurus* were also part of the Cretaceous Period group of dinosaurs. They were strong and mighty creatures. And every one of them disappeared at the end of the Cretaceous Period.

Ichthyosaurus

While dinosaurs dominated the land, ichthyosaurs ruled the sea. They were not dinosaurs, though. Instead, they are considered a marine reptile that appeared during the Triassic Period. The first ichthyosaurs were simple creatures that swam like eels do today. Gradually, they developed longer fins and became better swimmers. Eventually, they evolved into quick predators. The ichthyosaurs also grew much larger. Some skeletons have been discovered that show the creatures could have been more than 40 feet long. That's about the length of a school bus!

While they were reptiles, there is evidence that ichthyosaurs gave birth to live offspring, as whales do. Also similar to whales, they did not have gills—they breathed air. The mass extinction that wiped out the dinosaurs at the end of the Cretaceous Period did not kill the ichthyosaurs. They had gone extinct before the end of the Cretaceous Period. No one knows why.

END CRETACEOUS EXTINCTION

What happened this time? Paleontologists looked at a lineup of the usual suspects. Maybe more volcanoes caused it. Maybe climate change did it. Maybe an asteroid was the culprit. For a long time, no one agreed on what wiped out the non-avian dinosaurs. The theory that a massive asteroid hit Earth seemed ridiculous. Then, scientists discovered clues. They followed leads. They turned to their silent witnesses—the rocks. Everything pointed to the same suspect: an asteroid.

Outside the town of Gubbio, Italy, there are many limestone cliffs that used to be deep under water. Today, they are exposed. The rock was formed by layers of sediment. A man named Walter Alvarez (1940–) was studying the strata and noticed something interesting.

In one layer, he found many foraminifera fossils. They were everywhere. They represented thousands of years of diverse forams. Above this layer there was a mysterious clay layer. And above that? The forams were much smaller and there were a lot fewer of them.

This is the boundary between the end of the Cretaceous Period in the Mesozoic Era and the beginning of the Cenozoic Era. Called the K-Pg boundary, it is from about 66 million years ago—the same time the dinosaurs disappeared.

DID YOU KNOW?

Where there are flowers, there are bees. For a long time, scientists had evidence that suggested bees existed only as early as 65 million years ago. Newer evidence shows they may have evolved around the same time as flowering plants, 130 million years ago.

What is a Dinosaur?

The word *dinosaur* means "terrible lizard," but dinosaurs are not lizards! Both are reptiles though, which means they had common ancestors millions of years ago. Both lizards and dinosaurs laid eggs and both had spines and scaly skin. The biggest difference is in the structure of their skeletons. Think about how a lizard or crocodile walks. Their legs are splayed out to the side. When they move, they sort of waddle back and forth. Dinosaurs, on the other hand, had their legs under them. This different hip structure allowed dinosaurs to move faster than reptiles.

iridium: a metallic element that is found in only small amounts in Earth's crust, but is much more common in asteroids.

crater: a round pit caused by the impact of something.

ejecta: the material that is thrust into the air as a result of an impact or explosion, such as a volcano.

vaporize: to turn into a gas.

WORDS TO KNOW

In Spain, scientists found similar patterns in the rock layers. This told scientists that life on Earth was doing very well right up until 66 million years ago, when something dramatic happened.

Scientists began to pay more attention to the mysterious clay layer. It varied in thickness, but was found all around the world. Alvarez knew that he'd made a great discovery. But he didn't yet know what it meant. With the help of his father, he examined samples of the clay layer from Gubbio. Within the layer, they found a clue—**iridium**.

Iridium is a rare element found in Earth's crust. The mysterious clay layer contained large amounts of iridium. Not only that, but the clay had 30 times more iridium than the layers above and below it. The same was true at other K-Pg boundaries around the world.

Where could all that iridium have come from? Walter Alvarez's father came up with a hypothesis: an asteroid caused the mass extinction at the end of the Cretaceous Period. He then calculated how big the asteroid would have been. His estimate was that the asteroid was about 6 miles wide, the size of Mount Everest. It would have weighed hundreds of billions of tons. And it would have been traveling at almost 50,000 miles an hour.

DID YOU KNOW?

You can read more about the discoveries of Walter Alvarez and the investigative work he did with his father in this article. How did father and son work together to create hypotheses about what happened at the K-Pg boundary? The article explains their conclusions and describes what happened when an asteroid struck Earth.

PS

Day the Mesozoic Died 🔎

Could an asteroid 6 miles wide cause a mass extinction? Sure, everything in its path would be wiped out, but Earth is a big planet. Six miles might be the distance to your school or to your friend's house. Many scientists felt an asteroid of this size would not have caused a mass extinction. The father-and-son team continued their investigation. They had to find more evidence to prove their hypothesis.

One of the pieces of evidence they hoped to find was the impact **crater**. So far, no one had discovered a crater that was old enough and the right size to support the hypothesis.

Since more than two-thirds of Earth's surface is water, they wondered if the crater might be on the floor of the ocean. In that case, they might never find it!

Scientists knew that if an asteroid did hit Earth, a mass of debris, called the **ejecta**, would have blasted from the crater. If they could find the ejecta, that would support the hypothesis. When scientists looked at the strata at the K-Pg boundary again, they found bits of **vaporized** rock there. This rock would have been vaporized on the asteroid's impact, carried by the wind, and then fallen back to Earth. Eventually, it would have cooled and solidified. This vaporized rock provided an important clue.

Scientists also discovered shocked quartz at the K-Pg boundary. Shocked quartz forms only as a result of a violent explosion or impact, which deforms the quartz crystals into unique patterns. Comparisons of shocked quartz from the K-Pg boundary around the world revealed that the size of the shocked quartz increased closer to North America. Scientists were beginning to think that the crater must be close to the United States.

More evidence was found in Texas. In a riverbed, scientists found evidence of a massive **tsunami**. The force of the tsunami had ripped up the ocean floor and deposited it in its current location. This evidence told scientists that they were getting closer.

The breakthrough came from geologists looking for oil in the Gulf of Mexico. With high-tech instruments, they detected an enormous crater that was partly submerged in the ocean. The size of the crater matched Alvarez's predictions. The rock samples there were examined and found to be 66 million years old. Everything backed up the impact hypothesis. The crater was named the Chicxulub Crater.

Now that we have evidence of a massive asteroid hitting Earth, think back to the example of dominos in Chapter 2. How can you apply that model to the mass extinction caused by the asteroid?

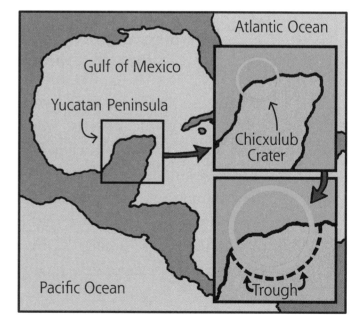

First, the asteroid struck Earth with enormous force. This caused earthquakes, tsunamis, and a shockwave of heat. A large region would have been as hot as your oven when it's broiling a steak. The asteroid would also have blasted massive amounts of ejecta into the air. As the ejecta rained down over a wide area, it would have caused wildfires. The smoke from the fires and the debris from the impact would have blocked out the sunlight for months.

Without sun, there is no photosynthesis. In addition, the matter in the air would have caused acid rain. The Earth cooled for a while. However, the gases released by the impact eventually caused **global warming**, resulting in extreme heat. The extreme climate changes caused ecosystems to collapse.

All of these dominos falling resulted in a mass extinction. Many dinosaur species disappeared. Many other species also went extinct. But some survived. We'll meet those species and see how they lived in the next era—the Cenozoic.

ESSENTIAL QUESTION

Now it's time to consider and discuss the Essential Question: What happened to the dinosaurs?

SPECIES SPOTLIGHT

Birds

Scientists have determined that birds are descended from dinosaurs. Does that mean a bird is a reptile? Sort of. They certainly don't look like dinosaurs or even reptiles. However, they lay eggs like reptiles and dinosaurs. And, they have scaly skin (look at a bird's foot!). Other evidence supports the theory that birds are distant cousins to dinosaurs, such as large eye openings in the skull. Birds also have hollow bones like some dinosaurs. But not all experts agree. Some say there isn't enough evidence in the fossil record. Others point to differences in the feet and ankles between birds and theropod dinosaurs. Like many things in ancient history, we may never know for sure.

Simulate an Asteroid Impact Crater

**Investigate what happens when an asteroid
strikes Earth by creating your own!**

You will need to find a good place for this experiment, such as a
sandbox or area of dirt. Find balls and rocks of different sizes and
weights. Pick a height from which you will drop your objects and start
making craters!

Drop one object. Measure the width and the depth of the crater.
Measure how far your "ejecta" travels. Record your answers in a chart in
your science journal.

	Trial 1	Trial 2	Trial 3	Trial 4	Trial 5
Diameter of Object					
Weight of Object					
Height of Drop					
Diameter of Crater					
Depth of Crater					
Pattern of Ejecta					

ACTIVITY

Smooth over the crater before you drop each new object. For the best comparison, you'll need to drop each object from exactly the same height.

You can take this experiment even further by performing it in a pool. You could use a baby pool or one in your neighborhood. This time, see if you can measure the size of the waves.

CONSIDER THIS: Which object made the biggest crater? Which was more of a factor, size or weight? You could also try the experiment from a different height to see if the results are different. Was there a pattern in the spray of ejecta? Using your math skills, can you calculate the volume of material that was ejected from the crater site? How much bigger than the object was the volume of displaced material? Another thing to consider is how high into the air the ejecta flew. Try recording the impact in slow motion to see the impact more closely.

ACTIVITY

Create a Strata Story

IDEAS FOR SUPPLIES

small objects, such as toys or coins ☺ 2 containers ☺
5 types of sediment, such as sand or gravel

Scientists read the layers of rock like pages of a book. Now it's your turn to tell a geologic story. You will need a friend, sibling, or adult as a partner. This activity requires you (and your partner!) to come up with a simple story you would like to tell. You will act as both storyteller and as story reader.

Start by determining the geologic story you want to tell. It can be based on real geologic events, such as a sea that gives way to a forest. Your story could be entirely made up or based on the timeline of your own life. The story could also be something funny. Whatever you decide, think of clues you will need to leave in five different layers of strata so your partner can "read" the story. Your partner should do the same.

Gather "fossils" to put in the strata. Use your imagination. You can use anything: small toys, shells, sticks, coins, bottle caps, acorns, etc.

Gather two empty containers. Collect five different types of sediment. You could try gravel, dirt, clay, sand, or dry rice.

Once you have your materials, cut the tops off the containers. Lay your first layer of sediment and fossils. The layer should be about an inch thick. Pack down the layer. Place the next four layers the same way. Remember that the first layer you place will be the "oldest." This is the beginning of the story.

DID YOU KNOW?

A fossil of feathers and part of a tail of a baby dinosaur was discovered in a piece of amber in 2016. Resin is a sticky substance that oozes from trees and amber is hard, fossilized resin. The amber keeps fossils as preserved as plastic would today.

Once you have finished with your strata, add some water. Pack down the layers. Now swap containers with your partner. Cut away one side of the container and start excavating. Take notes as you do.

Layer	Type of Sediment	Fossils Discovered	Thoughts/ Observations
1			
2			
3			
4			
5			

Try to write the story your partner was trying to tell. Share your findings with each other.

CONSIDER THIS: Were you able to read the story your partner was trying to tell? Did you have enough clues? Which clues were the most helpful? Were there gaps in the story? If you could not understand the story fully, could you make a guess based on the clues?

Paleontology Is Hard Work!

Paleontologists spend long days digging out fossils. They can be difficult to remove. Plus, scientists don't want to damage the fossils in the process. Get a glimpse into the work of a paleontologist using a chocolate chip cookie!

Once you have a chocolate chip cookie in front of you, your job is to remove the fossils (the chocolate chips!). You must do this without damaging the fossil or the ground (the cookie). And, the better you do, the more money you will "earn." Collect tools you think might be helpful to do this precise work.

Consider these costs and benefits while you work.

* For each complete fossil you excavate, you can earn $50.

* If you excavate part of a fossil, that's worth $20.

* If you break a fossil, you must pay $20.

* If you break the ground, you have to pay $20.

DID YOU KNOW?

"Understanding how we decipher a great historical event written in the book of rocks may be as interesting as the event itself."
—Walter Alvarez

CONSIDER THIS: What skills did it take to successfully excavate the fossils? What tools did you use? Did you go looking for different tools once you got started? Would you consider your "dig" a success? Why or why not? What might you do differently next time? You may want to try this activity again with someone else and work as a team. Does that make it easier or harder? How might working as a team benefit paleontologists in the field?

ACTIVITY

Chapter 4

THE CENOZOIC ERA

The end of the Mesozoic Era was the end of the non-avian dinosaurs. The giant reptiles became extinct. It was also the end of about 60 percent of all plant species. However, as we've seen, it was not the end of life on Earth.

After Earth's fifth mass extinction 66 million years ago, ferns were some of the first plants to recover, because they **germinate** more easily than flowering plants. Other animals filled the **niche** left by dinosaurs. These animals included turtles, birds, mice, and frogs, which are all small and reproduce quickly. Species of mammals evolved and became more diverse. After millions of years, they came to dominate the landscape.

? ESSENTIAL QUESTION

Is extinction a good thing or a bad thing?

germinate: to sprout and begin to grow.

niche: the way an organism fits into an ecosystem.

vertebrate: an animal with a backbone.

food web: a network of connected food chains that shows the complex set of feeding relationships between plants and animals.

trophic cascade: a chain reaction that occurs in an ecosystem when top predators are removed.

Pleistocene Epoch: a period of time during the Cenozoic Era that lasted from about 2,600,000 years ago to 10,000 years ago.

megafauna: very large animals.

marsupial: a type of mammal that has a pouch on the stomach of the female for carrying and nursing young.

WORDS TO KNOW

The Cenozoic Era is often called the age of mammals. While it's true that mammals thrived during this time, they weren't the only species to do well. Fish thrived, too. They succeeded because the other species that competed for food in the oceans died out.

Starting at the beginning of the Cenozoic Era, fish species began to diversify and grow larger. These ray-finned fish are the ones you probably think of when you think of fish. They include goldfish, cod, piranha, trout, barracuda, and more. All of these fish have a bony spine that supports their fins. Today, ray-finned fish are the most diverse **vertebrate** species.

Food Web

Have you ever heard of a **food web**? In a food web, there are the producers at the base. These are plants that make their own food through photosynthesis. Primary consumers eat them. Secondary consumers eat the primary consumers. This happens all the way up the chain to the top predators. What happens when links go missing? The whole food web is affected. When top predators, such as the dinosaurs, disappear, the effects are called a **trophic cascade**. This happens when a change at the top of the food chain affects everything at every level below it.

MEGAFAUNA

When we think of extinction, we often think of it as something negative. In the case of the dinosaurs, Earth lost its great beasts. But it's probably a good thing there's not an *Allosaurus* lumbering down your street right now. There's another reason, besides safety, to be grateful for the dinosaur extinction.

**After every extinction, other life thrives.
In this case, it included humans.**

After the dinosaurs died, some mammals in the Cenozoic Era gradually evolved into larger and larger animals. By the beginning of the **Pleistocene Epoch, megafauna** had evolved. This included giant ground sloths, saber-toothed cats, and mastodons in North and South America. There were also *Glyptodons*.

These animals looked like small cars with armored shells, similar to overgrown armadillos. Australia's megafauna included a carnivorous lizard more than 20-feet long, a 7-foot-tall kangaroo, and huge **marsupials**.

A species similar to gigantic rhinoceroses lived in Africa. In other parts of the world, there were woolly mammoths, cave bears, and even large, flightless birds that would have towered over a grown man. In the ocean, megalodons, similar to super-sized great white sharks, grew to be as big as 50 feet long with teeth that were 7 inches long. For a megalodon, a dolphin would have been a light snack.

comet: a ball of ice and dust that orbits the sun.

primitive: being less developed.

WORDS TO KNOW

As you know, there are few large beasts roaming the earth today. Most of the Pleistocene megafauna disappeared. What happened to them? They thrived for more than 100,000 years, all across the planet.

Their disappearance was not considered a mass extinction, but something wiped out these big beasts. And the case is still under investigation.

Another asteroid strike is a prime suspect. In Arizona, the rocks have revealed a layer called the black mat. It marks the time from 12,000 to 13,000 years ago. In that rock, scientists have found increased amounts of iridium. The amounts are not as great as when the dinosaurs were wiped out, but the layer is still unusual.

The problem is, though, we can't find the crater.

Some scientists have suggested that a **comet** broke up as it entered the atmosphere. In that case, the earth would have been hit by thousands of smaller pieces. Each would have made a dent in the land. Those smaller impressions could easily have been eroded or filled in during the next few thousand years.

Tree of Life

Evolution is a very complex subject, one that scientists learn more about every day. The Tree of Life web project was put together by biologists and nature lovers from around the world. The tree has a lot of information about the history of evolution. You can also learn how species are related and facts about certain species. There are even "treehouses" on the site just for kids where you can find investigations, stories, games, and more. Check it out at this website!

tree of life 🔍

Giant Ground Sloth

Imagine a sloth. Not a small, shy creature you might have seen in the zoo. No, imagine a sloth as tall as a giraffe and as round as an elephant. This was the size of the largest of all sloths, called *Megatherium*. It lived in North and South America from about 35 million years ago to about 11,000 years ago.

These gigantic, furry sloths could walk on two legs. They might have also used their tails as a tripod for stability. That was especially helpful when they tried to reach high into trees. Like the sloths of today, they were vegetarians. These giant sloths lived on the ground, not in the trees. They were too big!

Remember Georges Cuvier? He was the one to name the Megatherium. Around the time that Cuvier was studying the mastodon bones, the bones of the giant sloth were discovered in South America. Cuvier was convinced that it was another extinct species. Just like scientists today, Cuvier was unsure about the causes of extinction. He said, "What was this **primitive** earth? And what revolution was able to wipe it out?"

giant ground sloth

human

Another scenario sets the scene of the crime on the ice age glaciers. Simulations in labs show that a comet would have broken the ice into many pieces. The craters in the ice would have disappeared when the ice broke and melted, leaving no evidence behind. The search for evidence to support this hypothesis continues.

Other scientists don't agree that another asteroid was the culprit. First, there's no evidence of an impact event in North America big enough to affect megafauna on other continents. Also, many types of large animals were wiped out while other species were not.

Studies of glaciers point to a different suspect—climate change. The layers of ice in a glacier are similar to layers of rock. They provide a lot of detail about Earth's climate. One study of a **core sample** from a glacier in Greenland revealed evidence of the ice age that happened 12,000 years ago. The ice core revealed that the world froze very, very quickly—the temperature drop was dramatic. Still, the animals had survived other dramatic climate changes. Why would the one 12,000 years ago have killed them? And why did the temperature change happen so quickly?

There were other global climate changes toward the end of the Pleistocene Epoch that could have caused the extinction of the megafauna. The changes would have caused some habitats to expand and other habitats to shrink.

If the mega-beasts couldn't adapt, if the change was too quick, or if competition for resources increased, they would have been doomed to extinction.

A third hypothesis suggests that disease spread quickly when primitive people **migrated** to North America. The diseases they brought with them would have been new to North American fauna. The animals would not have had a natural **immunity**. They would not have been able to fight off the diseases. However, scientists have not found any evidence of disease in the bones of the mega-beasts. This theory also doesn't explain the megafauna extinctions in other parts of the world.

HUMANS EVOLVE

There is one more hypothesis about what killed the megafauna during the Pleistocene Epoch. Before looking at this last suspect, let's first discuss the evolution of another mammal— *Homo sapiens*.

About 60 to 65 million years ago, at the start of the Cenozoic Era, early **primates** evolved. This led to the evolution of monkeys, **apes**, and eventually humans. Yes, humans are primates! Between 5 and 7 million years ago, our evolution path split from an ancestor we share with apes.

DID YOU KNOW?

Humans share almost 99 percent of our DNA with two primates, chimpanzees and bonobos.

The evolution of modern humans can be difficult to understand. Remember, it didn't happen overnight—a chimpanzee didn't give birth to a human baby. The evolution took place through millions of years. During all that time, very small changes took place. For a while, early humans even had a combination of human- and ape-like features.

As with all species, humans evolved because of **adaptations**. One of those was the ability to stand and walk upright. This helped early humans spot danger in the grasslands of Africa where they lived. It also helped them survive. They became larger and stronger. Early humans also had larger brains than their ancestors. They were able to figure out how to use tools and make fire. This allowed them to communicate and plan, too.

Evidence shows that primitive humans began to make tools more than 3 million years ago. They began to use fire for cooking and heating between 1.8 million and 800,000 years ago.

The human brain also became more complex and humans developed language. They also began to migrate. From their origins in southern Africa, Homo sapiens moved to all corners of the earth.

The first documented humans in North America are called the Clovis People. Scientific evidence shows that the Clovis People arrived in North America just before the megafauna disappeared. They are the final suspect in the search for the North American megafauna killer.

Scientists have suggested that these humans were skilled super-predators. They had communication, weapons, and coordinated group hunting. These skills could have helped humans hunt the giant mammals to extinction. This theory is called the human overkill theory.

Could primitive humans really have killed entire species across the North American continent? Many scientists think not.

There is evidence of humans hunting mastodons and woolly mammoths, but what about other species? On other continents, the debate is similar. There is evidence that humans played a role in hunting these beasts to extinction, yet there is no proof that they were the entire cause.

No matter the reason, the megafauna are gone. As you've seen with other extinctions, the disappearance of one species leaves a niche open for other species to thrive. If that niche hadn't been opened, would other species have survived and evolved?

? ESSENTIAL QUESTION

Now it's time to consider and discuss the Essential Question: Is extinction a good thing or a bad thing?

What If . . .

It's time to make some predictions based on what you've learned about extinction. This activity is fun to do with a friend, sibling, or adult so you can share with each other.

Think about dinosaurs. What if they hadn't been wiped out by an asteroid 66 million years ago? What would the world be like today? Develop a hypothesis. For help, look outside the window. Focus your thoughts on what you see and how it would be different.

* Would the megafauna have evolved if the dinosaurs weren't wiped out by an asteroid?

* Would mammals have evolved at all?

* Would the dinosaurs have lived through an ice age?

* Would humans have evolved?

* What else might have evolved?

* What might have gone extinct?

* How would ecosystems have been affected if the dinosaurs had lived?

Once you've brainstormed, put your thoughts into a creative work. You could write a story, create a collage, draw a picture, or make a diorama.

CONSIDER THIS: If you share your work with someone, how is yours similar to theirs? How is it different? You might want to try the activity again, but this time imagine that the megafauna hadn't gone extinct. Or maybe that there is still an ice age.

Megafauna Food Web

When one species goes extinct, it can affect the entire food web. To get an idea of what happened after the megafauna went extinct, create a model of a food web.

Pick a species of megafauna that interests you. Do some research to find out where it lived and what it ate.

* Did it have any predators? Don't forget—humans were considered top predators!

Research the producers in the megafauna's food web. Then, research the other consumers in the ecosystem.

* Can you put together an entire web?

Create a presentation of the megafauna's food web.

* What is the top predator?
* What is the most basic producer?
* Where are there weaknesses in the food web?

CONSIDER THIS: Remember that a change in the population of one species in your food web will affect the populations of other species, including plants, animals, bacteria, and other organisms. Which species would benefit from the megafauna extinction? Which ones would suffer? How do you think the extinction of the species you chose affected the food web you created?

Human Ancestors

Back in the 1800s, people were outraged at the idea that humans evolved from primates. But you don't have to study DNA to understand the relationship. Careful observation reveals their similarities with humans. For this activity, have an adult take you to your local zoo. If you can't get to a zoo, see if you can find a documentary on apes. Ask an adult to help you find videos on the Internet.

Spend some time observing the apes, either live at the zoo or in a video. Make two lists, one that details the similarities to humans in terms of appearance and another that lists the actions and behaviors that are human-like.

Write a third list about how apes' appearance is different from humans'. For your final list, write down what you see about how apes act differently from humans.

* What are the similarities and differences between how apes and humans look?

* Which list is longer?

* Were you surprised by your close observations? Why or why not?

DID YOU KNOW? Apes cannot speak, but they can learn sign language! Some apes in captivity have learned hundreds of signs. And while they cannot form complex sentences, some have learned to put words together to communicate what they want.

CONSIDER THIS: Why might people not like the idea that humans and apes are related? How do you feel about that idea?

Chapter 5

SURVIVAL

Extinction happens all the time. Background extinctions are ongoing. There have also been mass extinctions that wiped out much of life on Earth at the same time. Yet even as extinctions are occurring, some species survive.

As you know, the idea that species went extinct wasn't something that humans even considered until the eighteenth century. People didn't think about species changing or evolving. But that changed when scientists began to observe the natural world closely.

? ESSENTIAL QUESTION

Why do some species survive while others do not?

theory of evolution:
a scientific theory that explains how species change through time and how they have all evolved from simple life forms.

natural selection:
one of the basic means of evolution in which organisms that are well adapted to their environment are better able to survive, reproduce, and pass their useful traits along to their offspring. Those organisms that are not well adapted are less likely to survive and reproduce, and the less useful traits die off.

WORDS TO KNOW

DID YOU KNOW?
If you think that turtles look prehistoric, you're right! The first turtles evolved more than 250 million years ago.

ADAPTATION

One man who spent a lot of time studying nature in the 1800s was Charles Darwin (1809–1882). Eventually, he began to wonder why some baby animals died and why others survived. Were the survivors just lucky? Was there something special about them? He found the answer when he started looking at the variations among individuals in a species.

Think about your family or a group of friends. You're all the same species—human. But there are many variations among you. Even within your own family, no two people are exactly alike. There are differences in how you look. Some people are tall, while others are short. Skin color and facial features vary. Some people might be fast runners and others are very coordinated. There could be some people in your class with great eyesight and others who can throw a ball with great accuracy.

Everywhere you look, there are variations among humans. There are variations within plants and animals, too.

Charles Darwin's observations of these variations led him to develop the **theory of evolution** by **natural selection**. Through his extensive research, Darwin learned that these variations within species are important to their survival.

Charles Darwin

In 1859, Charles Darwin published his work in a book titled *The Origin of Species*. He took 20 years to write it! During that time, he gathered facts and evidence. He wanted to make sure that his work was scientifically accurate. Darwin knew that some people wouldn't like that his theory suggested all living things on Earth were related to each other. Because of this, he knew his work would be criticized. Despite his careful scientific work, some people hated *The Origin of Species*. Some people even hated him! Still, Darwin succeeded in changing how people understood evolution. Why do people sometimes criticize the people who are doing the work instead of criticizing the work itself? To learn more about the life and research of Charles Darwin, visit this Darwin timeline.

Darwin timeline BBC 🔎

The individuals with useful variations that help them avoid predators or get food more easily are the ones that survive and reproduce. Then, they pass the useful variations onto their offspring through their DNA. The individuals that don't have useful variations aren't as likely to survive or reproduce.

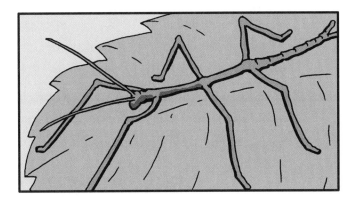

In this way, the variations that aren't helpful die out. The useful variations, though, are passed along from one generation to the next. These become adaptations of a species. Think about a stick bug. Have you ever seen one? Maybe not, because they are hard to see! It is hard for predators to see them, too. This is an example of a species well adapted to its environment.

WORDS TO KNOW

echolocation: finding things by sending out sound waves and listening for them to bounce back.

prey: an animal hunted by a predator for food.

scavenger: an animal, bird, or insect that eats rotting food or animals that are already dead.

nocturnal: active at night.

Other species have adaptations that help them find food, water, or shelter in their environment. Bats are a good example. They have developed their use of **echolocation** to catch insects. By using this method of sending and receiving sound waves, bats can pinpoint the location of their **prey**.

Plants adapt, too. In the desert, the creosote bush creates a toxin that keeps other plants from growing nearby. That way, the creosote bush gets more of the water and nutrients in the desert for itself!

The species that are well adapted to their environment survive. Species that are not become extinct.

Darwin also realized that, during a long period of time, a species might have a lot of adaptations. In fact, they might have so many that they don't look anything like their long-ago ancestors. All of these changes add up, creating a new species.

DID YOU KNOW?

At first, Darwin did not say directly that man shared an ancestry with apes. He wanted to be careful about how people thought of his work. It wasn't until 1871 that he published *The Descent of Man*, which suggested the evolution of humans from primitive ancestors.

ENVIRONMENTAL CHANGES

Changes in environment force adaptation. If the environment stays the same, species don't evolve much at all. But what happens if an environment changes and a species doesn't adapt? That's right—extinction.

SPECIES SPOTLIGHT

Cockroaches

Cockroaches are very persistent creatures! They are difficult to get rid of if they infest your house. Even mass extinctions can't get rid of them! In fact, cockroaches have survived the last three mass extinctions. That means species of cockroaches have been around for more than 350 million years. Today, they look about the same as they did when they first evolved. The only difference? During the Paleozoic Era they were twice the size of cockroaches today, about 3.5 inches long.

Cockroaches are extremely hardy. They will eat just about anything. If food sources change, they change their diet. They can go long periods of time without food or water, which comes in handy when food sources are scarce. They are also good **scavengers**. Cockroaches are **nocturnal**, so they stay out of sight of many predators. They also reproduce very, very quickly. One cockroach can have thousands of babies in one year. Today, there are more than 4,000 different species of cockroaches all around the world.

Most of the time, changes in the environment happen very slowly. Environmental changes can include warmer or cooler temperatures, loss of habitat, disease, loss of food sources, and more.

When these changes occur, many species already have the necessary variations to survive the change. These variations might include the ability to move to a new environment. Some species can change their diet if they need a different food source. Others can fight off disease. Some are not sensitive to temperature changes. Species that can't adapt or don't have the needed variation go extinct. This is normal background extinction that is happening all the time.

metaphor: a way to describe something by saying it is something else.

Industrial Revolution: a period of time beginning in the late 1700s when people started using machines to make things in large factories.

camouflage: colors or patterns that allow a plant or animal to blend in with its environment.

WORDS TO KNOW

During mass extinction events, the circumstances are different. The changes in environment are sudden. Think about a day when it was warm when you left for school, so you dressed in light clothes and didn't take a coat. Imagine that by the end of the day, a storm had rolled in. The temperature had dropped and it was raining or sleeting. This is a **metaphor** for what happened during mass extinction events. However, instead of being able to run home or catch a bus, species were stuck in this changed environment.

During such events, many life forms on Earth simply couldn't survive these massive changes. But some did!

SMALL BUT MIGHTY

What do cockroaches, frogs, and mice have in common? They're all small! It was often the smallest of species that survived extinction. The megafauna didn't survive the Ice Age and the hunting skills of human species. The dinosaurs didn't survive the asteroid impact.

This pattern continues back through the history of the earth. During the Devonian Period, massive marine creatures ruled the sea. After the extinction event that wiped out these giants, the vertebrates that had survived were much smaller. These vertebrates stayed small for millions of years.

Adaptation in Action

In 1848, most English peppered moths had greyish wings with black flecks. This allowed them to blend in with the light-colored lichen on the trees so they were protected from birds looking for a tasty treat. By the end of the century, most English peppered moths had darker wings! The reason had to do with the pollution from the **Industrial Revolution**. Pollution from factories and new forms of transportation, such as steam trains, affected the air quality. The lichen on the trees died as soot built up on tree trunks. This meant darker moths were better **camouflaged** and lighter moths became easy prey! The situation reversed again after clean air laws were passed in 1950. The lichen grew back on the trees and, eventually, most of the moths were the lighter color again.

image credit: Jerzy Strzelecki

After the asteroid event that killed the dinosaurs, again the survivors were small. They were the creatures that could **burrow**, including birds, frogs, and mice. The burrowing, both underground and in marine environments, allowed these creatures to escape from the intense heat that followed the asteroid impact. The dinosaurs had nowhere to go.

Plus, after the impact, there was little to no vegetation left. Earth was a wasteland. Even if dinosaurs survived at first, the food sources for large herbivores were nearly wiped out. Soon, the **carnivores** that depended on the herbivores as a food source began to suffer and die off. The food chain eventually collapsed.

The smaller creatures could find hidden food that other animals couldn't find.

Small species also need less to eat in the first place. A creature called *Thrinaxodon* was suited to survival. It was a small scavenger that was able to forage for small amounts of food and survive. *Thrinaxodon* did not perish in the Great Dying, but went extinct in the mid-Triassic period.

Another advantage for small animals is that they tend to have large populations. Compared to dinosaurs, there were a lot more of these small creatures alive when the asteroid hit. They reproduce more quickly, too. Think about animals you know today. A mouse can have a litter of 8 to 10 babies at one time. Plus, one mouse can have many litters every year.

Tardigrades

Tardigrades, also known as water bears, are no bigger than 1.5 millimeters in size. However, this micro-animal has survived all five mass extinctions! Not only that, they can be brought back to life after being dead for years. They have even been sent to space and survived. These tiny creatures can be found in the harshest environments on Earth!

After only a little more than a month, mice are mature enough to start having babies of their own! That makes a lot of mice.

Now consider bears, which are very different. A female grizzly bear must be between four and five years old to mate, and the litter is usually only two cubs. Oftentimes, these cubs do not survive to become adults. The female also takes care of the cubs for two to three years. During that time, she doesn't have more babies. As you can see, mice reproduce much more quickly than grizzly bears! The smaller species surely experienced many deaths during the extinctions, but there were enough of them that they could quickly reproduce and survive.

Understanding why some species go extinct and others do not is important. It allows us to address the threats to species that are at risk for extinction today.

ESSENTIAL QUESTION

Now it's time to consider and discuss the Essential Question: Why do some species survive while others do not?

Going on a Bear Hunt
IDEAS FOR SUPPLIES
microscope ☻ lichen or moss ☻ distilled water

Want to see prehistoric life? Go find a tardigrade! Tardigrades are microscopic animals that look a little bit like an eight-legged bear. They are among the hardiest of all species. You will need a high-powered microscope for this activity. If you don't have one at home, check at school or your local library.

Find a natural area. Look for lichen or moss growing on a rock or tree. It doesn't matter if it is dry or wet, warm weather or cold.

Collect a sample of the lichen or moss that you find. Soak the sample in distilled water for a day. Squeeze some of the water out of the moss over a plate or dish. Transfer the water to a microscope slide.

It may take some time to find a tardigrade. Look through the microscope for something moving. If you don't see anything after a minute, move the slide. When you do find something moving, focus on it. Tardigrades move fast, so you might need to adjust the slide. Have you found one? If not, be patient. Keep looking.

Make observations of your tardigrade in your science journal.

* What does it look like?
* How does it move?

* If you can find two together, how do they interact?
* Can you change their behavior?

CONSIDER THIS: Did you know that such creatures live all around you? Where else might they be living? How are they able to survive in all kinds of environments? Do you think they'd survive another mass extinction? What can we learn from them about adaptation?

What Would Survive?

Life on Earth has been around for a long time. It has survived mass extinctions and other changes. Think about how well everything is adapted to today's world. What if our world changed quickly?

Spend some time outdoors observing the life around you. Look at big things, such as people and trees. Observe smaller things, such as insects or small plants.

Imagine an asteroid impact at the South Pole or a mass volcanic eruption in Siberia. Predict how the species around you would be impacted.

* Which organisms would be the first to die?

* How would these deaths affect other creatures?

* Which species would survive the longest? How?

* What could you do to adapt to your new environment?

DID YOU KNOW?
Darwin's theory of evolution also stated that all species on Earth have evolved from simple life forms during millions of years.

CONSIDER THIS: How would the landscape around you change? What would survive an extinction event? What would recover first? Can you imagine a new species that might evolve?

Camouflage!

Gather some friends, siblings, or adults to explore camouflage in action! You will need at least three people.

This game is best played in the woods, but any outdoor area will do. Pick one person to be the predator. The other people are now the prey.

To start the game, the predator yells, "Camouflage!" That person must close their eyes and count slowly to 10. Meanwhile, the prey scatter and find a place to hide. The prey must be able to see the predator from their hiding place.

Once the predator reaches 10, they can open their eyes. However, the predator cannot move from where they are. The predator turns around in place and tries to spot the prey. If they spot someone, that prey is out.

The predator can look for prey for a couple minutes. Once they have found everyone, or cannot find anyone else, they hold up any number with their fingers. The predator must turn around one full time with their hand over their head showing the number. Once the predator has turned around one time, they yell for the prey to come out.

All prey that were not already "caught" come out. If they could see the predator and successfully recall the number the predator held up, they are a winner. They will survive another day!

CONSIDER THIS: What made some people better camouflaged than others? After you play a couple rounds of the game, do you learn how to adapt? Would you have worn a different colored shirt for the game? A hat? Are there some places that are better to hide than others? Did the predator learn the behavior of the prey?

Chapter 6

THE SIXTH MASS EXTINCTION?

As scientists investigate the megafauna extinction that happened 10,000 years ago, there is an important suspect in the lineup: humans. Humans are also responsible for many current extinctions. However, some people aren't convinced there's a problem.

Looking at background extinction rates for mammals, scientists estimate that one species goes extinct every 100 years. But in the last 100 years, there have been more than 40 mammal extinctions! If that keeps up, we could lose three out of every four species of mammals during the next 300 years. The same could be said of fish, birds, plants, and bacteria.

? ESSENTIAL QUESTION

Are we currently experiencing the sixth mass extinction?

There have been many studies done on this topic and scientists don't agree on exact numbers. However, they estimate that the current extinction rate is 1,000 to 10,000 times higher than normal. Many people are saying that we are currently experiencing the sixth mass extinction. They also say it's our fault.

TRANSFORMING EARTH

In the year 1600, there were approximately 600 million people on earth. By 2010, that number was close to 7 billion. Because of the increase in population, there is more demand for food, water, shelter, and energy. And, unlike most other species that came before us, we can completely transform our environment to meet these needs.

When we transform our environment, though, we sometimes destroy the habitats of other species. Think about the location of your favorite restaurant or your school or home. What used to be there? Was it **grasslands** or forests or **swamp**?

When humans build new structures and parking lots, we destroy the natural areas where many organisms live.

Habitat destruction forces native species to migrate or adapt. Some species don't make it. Panda bears are a famous example of a species threatened with extinction. Much of their habitat in China has been destroyed. Species in the United States that are threatened by habitat destruction include monarch butterflies, bumblebees, the black-footed ferret, and ferruginous hawks.

Habitat destruction also results in **fragmentation**. When we build roads and neighborhoods, we divide the wilderness into pieces. This means that instead of large areas to live in, species are confined to smaller, isolated fragments. In many cases, these areas are not large enough for species to roam, eat, and find mates.

Biological Dynamics of Forest Fragments Project

Due to the rapid **deforestation** in the Amazon rainforest, scientists are very worried about the species that live there. One project has focused on the impacts of fragmentation. This study was started in 1978 in the forests of Brazil. The Biological Dynamics of Forest Fragmentation Project (BDFFP) has learned a lot about the isolated forest "islands." One result of fragmentation is an increased number of edges. Instead of a huge, deep, dark forest, more light enters the forest. This has harmful effects on ground cover and on biodiversity. The work of BDFFP serves as a guide for conservation and land management.

Species that migrate are especially affected when this happens. The fragmented habitats don't always offer safe places to rest or secure **corridors** to pass through. On the outskirts of Santa Monica, California, mountain lions are in danger due to habitat destruction and fragmentation. It's as if these large cats are now stuck on tiny islands and cannot roam freely for food or shelter. These small areas can't support the natural populations of species.

Degradation is another type of habitat loss. This can be caused by **invasive species**, pollution, and disease. When humans bring new species from one place to another, invasive species upset native ecosystems. Everything gets out of balance.

SPECIES SPOTLIGHT

Dodo Bird

Mauritius is an island in the southwest part of the Indian Ocean. For many, many years, species thrived in the small, well-balanced ecosystem. One of those was a flightless bird called a dodo. It didn't matter that it couldn't fly, though. The dodo bird had no predators. The bird even laid its eggs right on the ground! The birds were big and could weigh up to 50 pounds. They stood about 3 feet tall. For comparison, consider that a goose weighs less than 20 pounds. The dodo bird went extinct when non-native species were brought to the island that preyed on the birds and their eggs.

Sometimes, non-native species take over the ecosystem. That's what happened on the island of Mauritius, when humans brought non-native species with them. The invasive species eventually killed the dodo bird.

In 1598, a fleet of Dutch ships discovered Mauritius. Soon there was a settlement on the island. And within 100 years, the dodo was extinct. The animals that humans brought with them became the dodo's predators. Pigs, goats, and rats ate the birds or scavenged the dodo's eggs.

Even though the extinction of the dodo was an accident, the fact that it was due to human forces was an omen of things to come.

Another way humans have degraded habitats is through pollution. Pollution includes litter, but it also includes the pesticides and fertilizers we put on crops, waste from mines, oil spills, and more. All of this pollution has an effect on the surrounding ecosystem and is often the cause of many deaths within that ecosystem.

DID YOU KNOW?

Giraffes were added to the IUCN Red List in 2016 as a species vulnerable to extinction. Giraffe populations have dropped 40 percent in 30 years. They are now rarer than elephants.

Sometimes, new diseases are introduced into an ecosystem. Humans ship species of plants and animals around the world. Sometimes, these animals carry diseases that the native species can't fight off. One example of this is the spread of a disease called chytrid fungus. This disease is wiping out frogs and other amphibians.

fossil fuels: coal, oil, and natural gas. These energy sources come from the fossils of plants and tiny animals that lived millions of years ago.

greenhouse effect: when gases such as carbon dioxide, methane, and water vapor permit sunlight to pass through but also trap solar radiation, causing the warming of Earth's surface.

average temperature: a number that mathematically represents the central or middle of all temperatures.

The golden frog in Panama, for example, used to be easy to spot. There was even a place nicknamed "Thousand Frog Stream" because there were so many frogs there. Now, the golden frog is on the International Union for Conservation of Nature (IUCN) Red List. According to the list, the frogs are critically endangered. Scientists are racing to capture and protect as many frogs as they can.

TRANSFORMING THE AIR

It is easy to see how humans have transformed the land. It's harder to see how we've transformed the air, but we have. People want energy to heat and cool their homes, to produce light to see by at night, and to power cars and other forms of transportation. We also need energy to power the factories that make clothing and cell phones and all of the things we use every day.

Most of the energy we use is produced by burning more and more **fossil fuels**. Burning those fuels emits gases, such as carbon dioxide, that trap heat from the sun in the earth's

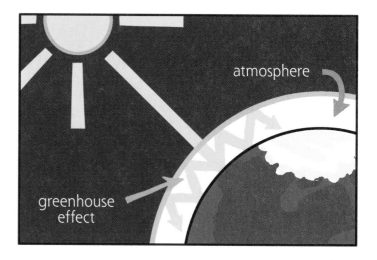

atmosphere. This creates a **greenhouse effect** on Earth that has caused temperatures to rise above historical levels. The result is global warming and climate change.

PS

IUCN Red List

If you want to know whether a species is extinct or threatened with extinction, you can look at the IUCN Red List. The IUCN is an organization of members from around the world who are dedicated to conservation. The Red List is the largest collection of information about the status of animal and plant species, collected to help guide global conservation efforts. The list is updated regularly.

IUCN red list 🔍

This rise in the earth's temperature is different from other changes you see day to day or between seasons. In this case, scientists look at the **average temperature**. Depending on where you live, the average temperature might be 50 degrees Fahrenheit (10 degrees Celsius). This measure takes into account those hot summer days and cold winter nights.

DID YOU KNOW?

Scientists calculated the levels of carbon dioxide in the air during the Great Dying, 250 million years ago. They also measured the level of carbon dioxide in the air today. The rate of carbon dioxide entering the atmosphere today is greater than it was during that mass extinction.

The location that has an average temperature of 50 degrees Fahrenheit this year might have had an average temperature of 48 degrees Fahrenheit (9 degrees Celsius) a few decades ago. That might not seem like a major difference, but even small changes in temperature can have a major impact on ecosystems and the species that live there.

The polar bear is an example of how temperature affects a species. The habitat of the polar bear is changing because the Arctic ice is melting faster than usual in the spring and isn't freezing until later than usual in the fall. The bears' natural hunting behavior is being challenged because of these changes, and food is scarce. As a result, the number of polar bears has the potential to decrease quickly. Scientists believe their numbers will continue to fall as Earth's average temperatures continue to rise.

Some people believe that this temperature change is natural. Earth's temperatures have been fluctuating for millions of years. More than 90 percent of scientists, though, do not agree that the current rapid global warming is part of the natural cycle. Instead, they have concluded that rising temperatures have been caused by human activity.

AQUATIC ECOSYSTEMS IN DANGER

Aquatic ecosystems have also been destroyed, fragmented, and degraded. Have you ever been to a reservoir or seen a dam? People create these structures to provide water for growing towns and cities, and for **agriculture**. But dams and reservoirs interrupt the natural flow of rivers and fragment the natural habitat. They also affect the amount of water in rivers.

DID YOU KNOW?

There can be invasive species in aquatic ecosystems, too. Zebra mussels hitched a ride on a ship from Europe in the late twentieth century. They are now threatening the whole Great Lakes ecosystem because they compete with native species for food and alter the habitat.

The Colorado River, for example, has its **headwaters** in the mountains of Colorado. It flows southwest through seven states. Along the way, there are numerous dams and reservoirs to hold back the water and provide it to more than 30 million people. By the time the river reaches the Pacific Ocean, there is often little or no water flowing.

Human activity affects the ocean, too. Remember that during the Permian extinction, massive amounts of carbon dioxide were spewed into the atmosphere? The oceans absorbed a lot of this carbon dioxide, which caused ocean acidification. Scientists are concerned that the same thing is happening today. Because of ocean acidification, shell species such as clams, mussels, and oysters can't produce and maintain healthy shells.

The world's coral reefs are also being affected. Corals are actually animals that build their own skeletons. In an acidic ocean, their growth is slowed and their skeletons are weakened. This makes them more vulnerable to erosion and predators. Not only that, but about 25 percent of all ocean species rely on coral reefs.

If the reefs die, the species dependent on the reefs might die, too.

There is another similarity between today's oceans and the Permian oceans. Today's oceans are warming and there are an increasing number of areas with little or no oxygen—scientists call these "dead zones." In these areas of reduced oxygen, many marine species can't survive. All of these factors threaten the balance of marine ecosystems around the world.

WORDS TO KNOW

marine debris: trash that ends up in the ocean.

decompose: to rot or break down.

sustainable: using natural resources at a rate that allows the resources to recover instead of being wiped out.

over-exploitation: the hunting or taking of a natural resource (such as animals or trees) faster than the population can reproduce, which often leads to extinction.

medicinal: having properties that can be used to treat illness.

There is pollution in the ocean, too. Some of this pollution is the result of oil spills. Some of it is because boats and ships lose cargo overboard. A lot of marine debris comes from land.

It might be hard to believe, but there are areas in the ocean called "garbage patches." These are places where ocean currents meet and the water swirls in a giant spiral. The marine debris that's carried by the current swirls, too, making a gigantic funnel of trash in the ocean. Most of this trash is plastic, which never decomposes. Instead, it breaks down into smaller and smaller pieces.

All marine species are affected by this debris. Sometimes, they become tangled in it.

Other times, they think the trash is food and try to eat it. Sea turtles, for example, feed on jellyfish, but often mistake plastic bags floating in the ocean for dinner. Sea birds also eat the plastic debris. On Midway Island in the north Pacific Ocean, albatross have been seen eating debris and feeding it to their chicks.

Researchers have found dead birds with stomachs full of plastic trash. Around the world, sea bird populations have dropped as much as 70 percent since 1950.

OVER-EXPLOITATION

Humans are top predators. With our tools and technology, we have designed ways to hunt and kill at a faster rate than any other species before us. Many people still rely on hunting as a source of protein for their families. These groups, however, tend to hunt only what they need. Their methods are sustainable.

Because of the increased population of people on Earth, there has been a growing demand for food, furs, tusks, and even exotic pets. This has resulted in the over-exploitation of many species. The list of species wiped out from over-exploitation includes the Pinta Island tortoise, the passenger pigeon, and the Steller's sea cow.

Most of the demands on animals do not arise from need. Shark-fin soup, for example, is a traditional dish in China. It is a symbol of wealth and is also thought to have medicinal value. However, the growing demand for the soup in China and in the United States has led to a collapse of shark populations.

On land, elephants are hunted for their ivory tusks, rhinos are killed for their horns, and tigers are hunted for their fur. None of these acquisitions are necessary for the survival of the human race, yet people continue to buy and sell these luxuries, even as the animal species is endangered.

DID YOU KNOW?

About 9 million tons of plastic trash end up in the ocean every year. That's the same as unloading a trash truck full of plastic into the ocean every minute.

poaching: the illegal
hunting and killing of
animals.

WORDS TO KNOW

Many species are protected by laws, but **poaching** continues. For some poor communities, the illegal hunting seems to be the only way to make money.

Wildlife crime affects all kinds of species, not just fish and mammals. Birds and plants are also illegally traded. This over-exploitation is not sustainable. If it continues, the world will see more and more species go extinct.

No species lasts forever. Yet, right now, species are going extinct much faster than normal. Is it happening fast enough that we should call it the sixth mass extinction? Scientists disagree about this. Some say it is too soon to call it a mass extinction. Others are convinced it's happening.

What do you think?

DID YOU KNOW?

African elephants could go extinct by 2040 if poaching continues.

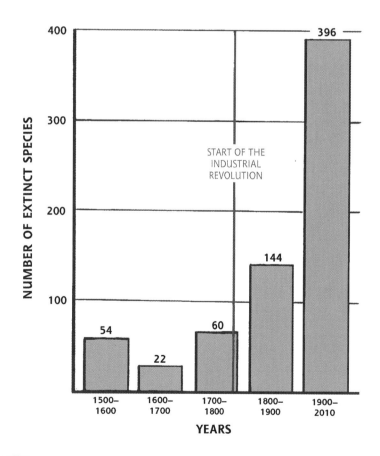

NUMBER OF EXTINCT SPECIES

400
396

300

START OF THE
INDUSTRIAL
REVOLUTION

200

144

100

60
54
22

1500–1600 1600–1700 1700–1800 1800–1900 1900–2010

YEARS

? ESSENTIAL QUESTION

Now it's time to consider and discuss the Essential Question: Are we currently experiencing the sixth mass extinction?

Three Out of Four

If scientists' predictions are right, three out of four species will go extinct during the next 300 years. What will the world be like? It's hard to imagine.

Spend some time in an outdoor space to get a better understanding of what scientists are predicting. You might choose your yard, a park, or outside your school. Make a list of the many different species you observe. Look all around you. Maybe even turn over some rocks, crawl in a garden, or climb a tree. Remember to include insects, mammals, birds, trees, and plants. Can you find 10 different species? Try for 20!

After you have your list, cross out three of every four of those species on it.

* Are any of the species you crossed off part of your food chain? What happens to the other organisms that rely on that species for food?

* What would you miss most about the species that you crossed off the list?

* How would the scene in front of you be different without those species?

* How might the other species change as a result of the extinction?

DID YOU KNOW? The year 2015 was the hottest since humans started keeping records in 1880. All of the 10 hottest years have occurred since 1998.

CONSIDER THIS: Draw the scene and species you observed. Then draw the scene again without the species you crossed off the list. What will happen to the ecosystem? What will the surviving species do for food and shelter? Do you think the ecosystem can be healthy, even with those missing species? Can some species adapt? What adaptations would they need to survive?

ACTIVITY

Reduce Your Carbon Footprint

Many things we do in the modern world require burning fossil fuels, such as driving a car, flying in an airplane to go on vacation, heating and cooling our homes, and using electricity. Not only that, most of the **manufactured** products we buy at stores were made in factories that burn fossil fuels. All of these activities release carbon dioxide into the atmosphere. This has led to global warming and ocean acidification.

There are things we can all do to help reduce carbon **emissions**. Start by visiting NASA's website about global climate change for students.

student climate change NASA 🔍

You can also visit its Household Carbon Footprint Calculator.

carbon footprint calculator 🔍

Read about the different steps you can take to help reduce climate change. Then make a plan and take action!

* What can you do to reduce carbon dioxide emissions?

* How might your actions help the health of the planet?

* What are some things you need to do to replace the actions and products that produce carbon dioxide emissions?

CONSIDER THIS: Think about a group of friends or a class at school. If you could get all of them to reduce their carbon footprints, calculate the total carbon emissions savings. Try to get one friend or classmate to join you in reducing carbon emissions.

WORDS TO KNOW

manufactured: made by machines.

emissions: something sent or given off, such as smoke, gas, heat, or light.

ACTIVITY

Create a Simple Air Pollution Detector

IDEAS FOR SUPPLIES

petroleum jelly ☻ notecards or paper plates ☻ magnifying glass

Sometimes, skylines are brown or hazy due to pollution. But most of the time, we can't see what's in the air. Yet, even if you can't see air pollution, it's there. As a result of human activity, air pollution is becoming a big problem. This simple activity will allow you to see what's floating around.

Find some petroleum jelly, often known as Vaseline. Spread a very thin layer of the jelly on several white notecards or paper plates.

Put your notecards in different locations, such as in the garage, in your kitchen, by the street, outside your school, and in your backyard. You might want to check the weather first! The cards need to stay in place for several days.

Check your cards every day and record what you see on them. Are some of them getting dirtier than others? What influence does the location have on the cards? After several days, collect your cards and label them with their locations. Study them with a magnifying glass. What do you see?

CONSIDER THIS: Rank them in order of cleanest to dirtiest. Which places were the most polluted? If your cards were dirty, what else might get dirty from air pollution? How do you think the pollution affects different species?

Bio-Plastic

IDEAS FOR SUPPLIES

three banana peels ๑ vinegar ๑ honey ๑ water ๑ thyme ๑ cinnamon

One of the greatest sources of ocean pollution is plastic. Not only that, but plastic does not biodegrade, so it accumulates in the oceans. To change this, many activists are calling for a reduction in plastic production. In addition, scientists are looking for more efficient ways to recycle plastic. They are also exploring the possibility of making plastic out of plant material instead, so that it will biodegrade easily. You can even do this yourself!

Caution: An adult must help with the boiling water.

Cut the banana peels into smaller pieces, then blend them with 1 cup of water. Ask an adult to help you heat the mixture in a small pot for five minutes over a medium heat. Stir occasionally as it heats. Just as it begins to boil, remove from heat. Add 1 cup more of water and stir.

Using a sieve, strain the mixture to get rid of the extra water. Press on the mixture to squeeze out even more water. Measure out 1.4 ounces of the mixture and return to the pot. Add the following:

* 4 teaspoons vinegar
* 1 teaspoon honey
* 1 teaspoon of cinnamon
* 1 teaspoon of thyme

Turn heat to medium again, and stir as the mixture heats. Remove before it burns or boils.

DID YOU KNOW?

Coral reefs are sometimes called the rainforests of the sea. They provide food and shelter for about 25 percent of all ocean species, including fish, turtles, jellyfish, crabs, octopuses, and clams.

WORDS TO KNOW

biodegrade: to break down or decay and become absorbed into the environment.

ACTIVITY

Turn the mixture out onto a piece of tin foil. Flatten the mixture. Then, put the flattened mixture, still on the tin foil, into the oven set to 125 degrees Fahrenheit (50 degrees Celsius) for 45 minutes to dry.

CONSIDER THIS: What does your bio-plastic look like? Feel like? Does the plastic look like you expected it to look? Why or why not? Does it seem strong enough to make everyday items out of?

If you tried this again, what might you do differently? What other natural materials might be used to make plastic?

Look around your house at all the things that are made of plastic. Do you think it's possible to completely change how we make plastic so that everything is biodegradable? Do some research to find out what solutions scientists are coming up with. Do you discover anything surprising in your research? How important is this issue?

The Life of Trash

Much of the trash that you throw away will outlive you, especially glass, plastic, and aluminum. That's because these manmade items don't break down very easily. And remember, plastic doesn't ever decompose entirely, it just breaks down into smaller and smaller pieces. Next time you throw something away, think about how long it will be around!

- › Glass Bottle, 1 million years
- › Plastic Beverage Bottles, 450 years
- › Aluminum Can, 80–200 years
- › Plastic Bag, 10–20 years
- › Cigarette Butt, 1–5 years
- › Apple Core, 2 months
- › Newspaper, 6 weeks
- › Orange or Banana Peel, 2–5 weeks

TAKING ACTION

In your lifetime, hundreds of species will go extinct. According to scientists, most of these extinctions will be the result of human activity. Experts who are trying to slow extinction rates cite many reasons for other people to join the fight.

The first reason is our own health. Plant and animal species have always helped humans find cures or treatments for diseases. People with heart conditions and childhood leukemia are treated with medicines that come from plants. What if the rainforest holds the cure for cancer? It's possible! It is also possible that plant species hold answers to curing or treating many other diseases and ailments.

? ESSENTIAL QUESTION

Why is it important to try to change human behavior to save species from going extinct? What can we do to slow extinction rates and the destruction of habitats?

Another reason to help keep species from going extinct is to protect biodiversity and ecosystems. If one species goes extinct, the entire food web could be impacted. And when ecosystems are unstable, they can collapse, resulting in more extinctions.

Other people simply believe that we should protect nature to preserve its beauty. When biodiversity decreases, ecosystems collapse. We lose beautiful and wild places on Earth forever.

Finally, there are those who believe that we have an **ethical** responsibility to save lives. They say many extinctions are human-caused. For that reason, humans have a responsibility to act to save species from extinction.

How can we stop what's happening?

It's a big, big world. It might seem like too much damage has been caused already. While that may be partly true, many scientists are optimistic that we have the tools we need to slow extinction rates. We just need to use those tools to do it.

DID YOU KNOW?

"The Earth does not belong to man; Man belongs to the Earth. This we know. All things are connected like the blood which unites one family. Whatever befalls the Earth befalls the sons of the Earth. Man did not weave the web of life, he is merely a strand in it. Whatever he does to the web, he does to himself."
—Chief Seattle (1786–1866), a Native American chief

HABITAT CONSERVATION

Around the world, many organizations have dedicated themselves to conservation. You may already know about the Sierra Club in the United States. It was founded by naturalist John Muir (1838–1914) in 1892 to protect our wilderness areas.

Have you ever been to one of the many national parks in the United States? The system of parks and monuments was established to preserve our natural resources. Not only do these places allow for the protection of the natural environment, they also provide educational experiences for the millions of people who visit them every year.

The United States and many other countries do a good job at setting aside land to protect it. But there is still work to be done. As of 2016, only about 15 percent of the land on Earth is protected. Some say we should increase that to 50 percent!

There are other conservation efforts focused on setting aside protected areas in the oceans, especially around coral reefs. In the United States, the National Marine Sanctuary System manages 13 marine-protected areas. These areas help to protect and restore marine ecosystems. They provide sanctuaries for a wide variety of marine species.

Other efforts around the world are also protecting parts of the oceans. People are working to restore damaged habitats, reduce pollution, and to promote sustainable fishing.

DID YOU KNOW?

As of 2008, there were more than 120,000 protected areas of land and ocean on Earth. That adds up to about 8 million square miles, which is twice the size of Canada.

Ross Sea

The Ross Sea is a deep bay in Antarctica. It is also one of the few places on Earth mostly untouched by human activity. Because of that, people have called it the "Last Ocean." At the end of 2017, it was set aside as the largest marine reserve in the world. The area under protection is the size of the country of Mongolia. It will serve as a sanctuary for penguins, whales, and 16,000 other marine species. The protection is the result of cooperation between many countries dedicated to preserving ocean places.

Another method of conservation is called **rewilding**. This is when large mammals are brought back to an ecosystem where they once lived. The hope is that by restoring the species, the whole ecosystem can be restored.

In Spain, for example, wild horses were reintroduced to the grasslands of the Campanarios de Azaba Reserve starting in 2012. The horses had lived in that ecosystem until humans began farming there. Now, the hope is that the horses will help sustain a healthy, natural grassland ecosystem.

In the United States, wolves were returned to Yellowstone National Park. Wolves had been hunted, trapped, and poisoned to extinction in the lower 48 states. Yet, because wolves are a top predator, the loss of the species caused instability in that ecosystem. They were reintroduced to the area in the mid-1990s. Since then, the ecosystem has stabilized, thanks to the wolves.

ecotourism: tourism that supports conservation efforts and promotes wildlife education.

WORDS TO KNOW

SPECIES CONSERVATION

In addition to protecting ecosystems, there are many efforts underway to help individual species. In Indonesia, for example, traditional manta ray hunts were a longtime part of the culture. The local people also made their living this way. However, the demand for the gills, meat, and skin of the rays became so great that the species populations dropped.

To save the rays, conservationists had an idea.

A fishing village relied on the rays for income. But what if the village could make money from tourism instead? That way, instead of killing the rays, the village could bring in tourists. **Ecotourism** can be a sustainable way to create jobs for villagers. The manta rays were protected and tourists got the unique opportunity to swim with these amazing creatures.

There are other efforts around the world to stop the wildlife trade. If the demand for ivory can be lowered, the elephants can be saved. If shark fin soup and animal furs become unpopular, poachers will be forced out of business.

How Wolves Change Rivers

What happens when you introduce a species back into its original environment? Sometimes, the results are surprising. When wolves were reintroduced into Yellowstone National Park, wildlife experts were amazed at what happened to the other species of plants and animals—even the rivers were changed! Watch this video to see what happened to the park ecosystem when the wolves were brought back.

wolves Yellowstone 🔍

Hawaiian Monk Seal

Hawaiian monk seals look a lot like other seals. Yet, unlike other seals, which like cold water, the Hawaiian seals like the tropics! They live near the northwest Hawaiian Islands. There, they swim and dive for fish, octopuses, and eels in the coral reefs. They can grow to be more than 7 feet long and weigh 600 pounds.

This species is facing extinction. The Marine Mammal Center reports that there may be fewer than 1,200 still alive. This number drops every year. The seals are at risk because humans also love warm, tropical areas. As a result, much of the monk seals' habitat has been degraded or destroyed. Fishing has hurt the population, too.

One conservation effort is protecting resting grounds. The seals swim, play, and hunt in the ocean, but need to come to shore to rest. When they do, volunteers rope off the areas where the seals are. They post signs asking people not to approach or bother the seals. There was also a rehabilitation hospital built on Hawaii in 2014. The hospital rescues sick and injured seals. The goal is to return seals to the wild once they are healthy again.

image credit: U.S. Fish and Wildlife Service

While many people are working to preserve species in the wild, for some species, it's too late. In these cases, efforts are aimed at capturing the last remaining members of a species to keep them alive in captivity. In 2017, one such effort was underway to save the last remaining vaquita porpoises in the Gulf of California, Mexico. To do this, conservationists had to locate, capture, and move the porpoises. The hope is to enclose them in a large floating pen or protected bay where they would no longer get caught up in fishing nets. The capture program is a collaborative effort by the Mexican government and other organizations.

THE ROLE OF SCIENCE

Conservationists aren't the only ones working to fight extinction. They've teamed up with **engineers** to find solutions. Scientists believe that one of the greatest challenges we face is global warming. The changing climate is threatening many species and habitats. One way to slow down this change is to stop burning fossil fuels and to use clean energy instead.

Engineers are working on ways to improve the function of solar energy cells and other methods of storing solar energy. They are researching ways to create **biofuel** for cars and other forms of transportation. Wind energy farms are also increasing in number. Engineers around the world are trying to find new, creative ways to lower **greenhouse gas** emissions.

DID YOU KNOW?

More than 200 endangered plants and animal species survive in our national parks.

Other engineers are coming up with a kind of artificial wood that can be used instead of trees to help stop **clear-cutting** of forests. Chemical engineers are trying to find pesticides for farmers to use that will protect crops without harming wildlife. These are just some of the many ways that environmental scientists and engineers have teamed up. Together, they are working to protect habitats and combat extinction.

There is another idea out there that has people talking. It's called "de-extinction."

Thanks to advances in science, it might become possible to bring species back from extinction. All they need is DNA. Using DNA from an extinct species, scientists might be able to recreate it.

In 2003, scientists successfully recreated a Pyrenean ibex, a species that had gone extinct three years earlier. While the recreated ibex didn't live long, scientists are hopeful that more research will bring species back from extinction.

Even if we can perform this procedure, should we? Some people believe that because so many extinctions were caused by human activity, it is our duty to correct that mistake. Others believe that bringing species back from extinction might cause problems in current ecosystems.

Despite this debate, scientists in California are collecting DNA from as many living species as they can. They are creating what is called the Frozen Zoo. At this "zoo," DNA samples are collected, labeled, and frozen. The scientists at the zoo hope to preserve life before it disappears.

EDUCATION AND AWARENESS

Education is another important part of slowing extinction. The more people are aware of the issues, the more they can do to help. A film called *Racing Extinction* was released in 2015. A team of artists and activists worked together to show the world the issue of mass extinction and endangered species. The goal of the filmmakers is to inspire people to act.

They wanted to spread the word that each action might seem small by itself, but if lots of people work together, we will make a difference.

PS Seafood Watch!

To make informed choices about the seafood you eat, you need to know where it comes from. The Monterey Bay Aquarium in California has designed an app to help you choose to buy seafood that has been harvested sustainably. The app is free and will help you and your family eat ocean-friendly seafood.

You can also browse its website (seafoodwatch.org) for information about good seafood choices and issues facing the ocean's health.

You can get the app here.

Seafood Watch 🔍

Part of making a difference is knowing the impact you have on Earth. For example, did you know that what you choose to eat for dinner has an impact on the environment? Not ordering shark fin soup is a good start. Avoiding or limiting how much beef you eat is important, too. The meat industry produces more greenhouse gases than the transportation industry! Make sure your seafood is a product of sustainable fishing. This protects fish populations and ocean ecosystems.

Talk to family members about unplugging devices when they aren't in use and turning off lights when they aren't needed. Think about driving less. Talk to your family about walking and biking more often or using public transportation. Every trip you save reduces the amount of carbon dioxide in the atmosphere. Imagine if every family at your school chose to leave their cars at home one day a week. The savings would start to add up!

Preventing extinction and climate change only happens when individuals take action. Sometimes, people work together as a group or for an organization. Others work alone. It's up to you. As Abraham Lincoln said more than 150 years ago, "You cannot escape the responsibility of tomorrow by evading it today."

? ESSENTIAL QUESTION

Now it's time to consider and discuss the Essential Question: Why is it important to try to change human behavior to save species from going extinct? What can we do to slow extinction rates and the destruction of habitats?

Start a "No Puffing" Campaign

On your way to school or the park or the store, look around. Do you see people sitting in their cars with the engines running? Have you seen cars warming up on cold days with no driver inside? This is called puffing. As you know, car exhaust pollutes the atmosphere. Is this a problem where you live? You can help!

Think about how you could start a campaign in your neighborhood or at your school to raise awareness. You might want to begin by researching the pollutants in car exhaust and their effects. Does restarting a car use more gas than letting it idle? Be informed of the science involved in puffing.

Once you've gathered the information you need, what should you do with it? How can you inform other people in your community about the effects of puffing? Brainstorm ideas in your science journal. You might want to form a committee made of friends and other students to help with your campaign.

DID YOU KNOW?

Air pollution from car exhaust is not only bad for the atmosphere. It is also harmful to human health. It has been linked to asthma, bronchitis, heart disease, and cancer.

CONSIDER THIS: After you've launched your campaign, take time to think about the difference you've made. Can you estimate the potential emissions reduction at your school or in your neighborhood? What went well with your campaign? How could you improve your campaign if you were to do it again or do another campaign? Are there ways to extend your campaign?

ACTIVITY

Recycled Paper
IDEAS FOR SUPPLIES
shredded paper old blender window screen frame

One of the greatest reasons for habitat loss is deforestation. Some of this is done for agriculture or development. Forests are also cut down to make paper products. The more we recycle paper, the more trees we keep from being cut down.

Many places have recycling programs, but you don't need big machines to recycle paper. You can do it at home. Collect some paper you would normally put in the recycling bin. Shred it with your hands and let it soak in water overnight or longer. Then mix it up with a hand-held beater, old blender, or other tool to create pulp. It will look a bit like oatmeal. The longer the pulp sits and the more you mix it, the better.

Create a frame to strain your pulp and remove the water. With an adult's permission, research on the Internet different ways to do this and the materials that you'll need. Think of it like creating a small frame that has a window screen nailed over it. Pour the pulp onto the screen and spread it out evenly. After it has dried out some, you can turn it out onto a tray or other surface to finish drying.

CONSIDER THIS: How did your paper turn out? Was it too thick? Too thin? What would you do next time to improve your recycled paper? Could you add decorative items to the pulp, such as glitter, seeds, or other items, for a different effect? What do you think is different about the commercial process that creates the recycled paper that we use?

Create a Green City

Imagine that you have been named the head engineer for a new town. All that's there right now is a mix of grassland and forest. Your job is to make the new town as green as possible. You will need to find a way to balance the needs of humans and the needs of the environment and the plant and animal species that live there.

Do some research on what makes a city green. Are there other cities that have been successful in going green? Make a list of things you will need to include in your new town to make it green. Also consider all the things in a town that people need—homes, schools, food stores, etc. Where will people work? Is there anything about the town you live in that you'd want to include or omit in your imaginary town?

Time to design it! How will you present your ideas for the new town? You might want to make a collage, create a model, make a diorama, or simply draw your new town. Gather all the supplies you'll need and set to work, paying attention to the green details.

CONSIDER THIS: Share your new town with family or friends. What are some of their responses? Explain why you excluded certain elements in your town. Are there aspects of it that you are especially proud of? Are there some things you might do differently next time? Was it difficult to balance the needs of the environment with the needs of people? Engineers, architects, environmentalists, and other scientists are important when creating green cities. Who might you talk to for more information?

WORDS TO KNOW

green: in conservation, to be environmentally friendly and sustainable.

Interconnected Waterways

IDEAS FOR SUPPLIES

cardboard egg carton ☙ *food coloring* ☙ *uncooked oatmeal or other small, powdery material* ☙ *water*

Ever wondered why you should be concerned about pollution in waterways hundreds of miles from you? Or maybe you don't think pollution or litter in one area could affect other areas, or even the ocean. This simple activity will give you an idea of how all waterways are connected—not only to each other, but also to the surrounding environment.

This activity is best done outside or over a tub! Fill the egg carton with water so that the water pours from one cup to the other.

Now, throw some oatmeal into one of the cups. This is your "litter." What do you notice? What happens if you keep adding more?

Add some drops of food coloring to a different cup. What happens? Let the water sit in the carton for a while. What is happening?

CONSIDER THIS: Think about how all waterways are connected, including creeks, rivers, lakes, and oceans. How is this similar to the water in the egg carton? Imagine if the dye you put in the carton was actually chemicals or waste in a lake. What would happen to the surrounding waterways? To the ground and environment around it? You may want to continue the activity by having it "rain" on one of the polluted cups. Or perhaps create a windstorm or earthquake!

ACTIVITY

What's Your Opinion?

Write an opinion piece for your school or local newspaper about what you see going on around you that is affecting the environment.

For best results pick one issue. Have you noticed litter or other pollution in a local stream or lake? Maybe you know of an endangered species nearby. Do research to back up your opinion with facts. Think about what the opposite side may think and find facts to discredit their argument.

Once you've written your piece, have a friend or adult read it and give you editing advice. After editing your piece, consider where you may want to share your piece. Newspapers are only one possible place to publish your opinion. If you have access to social media, you could post your piece with an adult's permission. Or you could email it to friends and family. You could also create a newsletter to hand out to people.

CONSIDER THIS: What did you learn about environmental issues in your area? Were you surprised? Do you feel that expressing your opinion about the issues facing species is enough? Are you motivated to do more? What action could you take concerning the issue you wrote about?

The Photo Ark

National Geographic and a photographer named Joel Sartore are creating an ark. It's not made of wood and it won't sail. The Photo Ark is an effort to photograph every species in captivity. Sartore wants to make a photo archive of the biodiversity on Earth before it's too late. He's up to almost 6,000 species. He wants to photograph every species in captivity to give each creature a voice. He also wants his work to draw attention to the extinction crisis. "I want to get people to care, to fall in love, and to take action," he says. You can view many photos from the Photo Ark at his website.

Joel Sartore 🔍

ACTIVITY

absolute age: a more precise age of rocks or fossils determine by radioactive decay.

acidic: from acids, which are chemical compounds that taste sour, bitter, or tart. Examples are vinegar and lemon juice. Water also contains some acid.

adaptation: changes an animal or plant makes (or has made) in response to its environment.

adapt: to make changes to better survive in an environment.

agriculture: the act of farming, growing crops, and/or raising animals for food or other products.

algae: a simple organism found in water that is like a plant but without roots, stems, or leaves.

amphibian: a cold-blooded animal, such as a toad, frog, or salamander, that needs sunlight to keep warm and shade to stay cool. Amphibians live on land and in the water.

ancestor: someone from your family who lived before you.

ape: a large, tailless primate such as a gorilla, chimpanzee, or orangutan.

aquatic: having to do with water.

archipelago: a group of islands.

arthropod: an invertebrate animal with a segmented body and limbs with joints, such as a spider or insect.

asteroid: a small, rocky object orbiting the sun. Asteroids are too small to be planets.

atmosphere: the mixture of gases surrounding Earth.

average temperature: a number that mathematically represents the central or middle of all temperatures.

background extinction: the ongoing, normal process of species going extinct.

bacteria: tiny organisms found in animals, plants, soil, and water.

beneficial: having good or helpful results.

biodegrade: to break down or decay and become absorbed into the environment.

biodiversity: many different species of plants and animals living in an area.

biofuel: fuel made from living matter, such as plants.

body fossil: a fossil that is formed from the hard parts of an animal or plant, such as bones, teeth, shells, or tree trunks.

boundary: in geology, the strata in the rock that marks the end of one period and the beginning of another.

breed: to produce offspring.

burrow: to dig underground holes and tunnels.

Cambrian Period: the first period of the Paleozoic Era, marked by an explosion of life.

camouflage: colors or patterns that allow a plant or animal to blend in with its environment.

carbon dioxide: a colorless, odorless gas. It forms when animals breathe and when plants and other living matter die and rot.

carnivore: an animal that eats other animals.

carnivorous: describes a plant or animal that eats only animals.

cell: the basic building block for all life on Earth.

clear-cutting: to remove every tree from an area.

climate change: a change in the long-term average weather patterns of a place.

comet: a ball of ice and dust that orbits the sun.

coniferous: describes cone-bearing shrubs and trees, often with needles for leaves. Coniferous trees do not lose their leaves each year.

conservation: managing and protecting natural resources.

coprolite: fossilized poop.

core sample: a section from deep within something, such as a tree or glacier, that is taken by drilling for scientific investigation.

corridor: a passageway or route to pass through.

crater: a round pit caused by the impact of something.

cyanobacteria: a type of aquatic bacteria that produces oxygen through photosynthesis.

debris: the pieces left after something has been destroyed.

decompose: to rot or break down.

deduce: to make a logical conclusion based on evidence.

deforestation: the act of completely cutting down and clearing trees.

degradation: the act of ruining or damaging something.

diversify: becoming more varied.

DNA: deoxyribonucleic acid. The substance found in your cells that carries your genes, the genetic information that contains the "blueprint" of who you are.

echolocation: finding things by sending out sound waves and listening for them to bounce back.

ecosystem: a community of living and nonliving things and their environment. Living things are plants, animals, and insects. Nonliving things are soil, rocks, and water.

ecotourism: tourism that supports conservation efforts and promotes wildlife education.

ejecta: the material that is thrust into the air as a result of an impact or explosion, such as a volcano.

emissions: something sent or given off, such as smoke, gas, heat, or light.

endangered: a plant or animal species with a dangerously low population.

engineer: someone who uses math, science, and creativity to solve problems or meet human needs.

environment: everything in nature, living and nonliving, including plants, animals, soil, rocks, and water.

epoch: a division of time within a period.

era: a division of geologic time.

erosion: when land is worn away by wind or water.

ethical: doing the right thing.

evolution: the theory of how species develop from earlier forms of life, through natural variations.

evolve: to gradually develop through time.

exoskeleton: a hard shell or cover on the outside of an organism that provides support and protection.

extinction: when the last living member of a species dies.

extirpated: to be completely missing from a certain area a species used to occupy.

food chain: a community of animals and plants where each different plant or animal is eaten by another plant or animal higher up in the chain.

food web: a network of connected food chains that shows the complex set of feeding relationships between plants and animals.

foraminifera: single-celled marine organisms with shells, also called forams.

fossil: the remains or traces of ancient plants or animals left in rock.

fossil fuels: coal, oil, and natural gas. These energy sources come from the fossils of plants and tiny animals that lived millions of years ago.

fossil record: the total number of fossils found in the rock layers.

fragmentation: the act of breaking something into smaller sections or pieces.

generation: a group born and living at about the same time.

geologic time: the span of Earth's history marked by major events and changes.

geologist: a scientist who studies geology, which is the history and structure of Earth and its rocks.

germinate: to sprout and begin to grow.

glacial deposit: big rocks or stones left when a glacier moves or melts.

glacier: a semi-permanent mass of ice that moves very, very slowly down a mountain or slope.

global warming: the long-term, overall rise in temperatures on Earth.

grassland: a large area of land covered with grass.

gravity: the force that pulls objects toward each other and holds you on Earth.

Great Oxygenation Event: the introduction of oxygen into Earth's atmosphere more than 2 billion years ago.

green: in conservation, to be environmentally friendly and sustainable.

greenhouse effect: when gases such as carbon dioxide, methane, and water vapor permit sunlight to pass through but also trap solar radiation, causing the warming of Earth's surface.

greenhouse gas: a gas such as water vapor, carbon dioxide, carbon monoxide, or methane that traps heat and contributes to warming temperatures.

habitat: the natural area where a plant or animal lives.

habitat destruction: destroying ecosystems to the point they can no longer support native species.

headwaters: the beginning point or source of a river.

herbivore: an animal that eats only plants.

Homo sapiens: the Latin word for the species of today's humans.

ice age: a period of time when ice covers a large part of Earth.

igneous rock: rock that forms from cooling magma. Magma is melted rock below the surface of the earth.

immunity: the ability to resist a certain disease.

impact event: when objects from outer space hit Earth.

Industrial Revolution: a period of time beginning in the late 1700s when people started using machines to make things in large factories.

invasive species: species that do not naturally belong in an ecosystem and may cause it harm.

invertebrate: an animal that does not have a backbone. A vertebrate is an animal with a backbone.

iridium: a metallic element that is found in only small amounts in Earth's crust but is much more common in asteroids.

lava: hot, melted rock that has risen to Earth's surface.

mammal: a type of animal, such as a human, dog, or cat. Mammals are usually born live, feed milk to their young, and usually have hair or fur covering most of their skin.

manufactured: made by machines.

marine debris: trash that ends up in the ocean.

marine: of or relating to the ocean.

marsupial: a type of mammal that has a pouch on the stomach of the female for carrying and nursing young.

mass extinction: when a great percentage of organisms go extinct within a short period of geologic time, thought to be the result of a global disaster.

massive glaciation: the widespread formation of sheets of ice.

medicinal: having properties that can be used to treat illness.

megafauna: very large animals.

metaphor: a way to describe something by saying it is something else.

microorganism: a living thing that is so small it can only be seen with a microscope.

migrate: to move from one place to another.

minerals: a naturally occurring solid found in rocks and in the ground. Rocks are made of minerals. Gold and diamonds are precious minerals.

mutation: a permanent change in DNA.

native species: a species that naturally belongs in an ecosystem.

natural selection: one of the basic means of evolution in which organisms that are well adapted to their environment are better able to survive, reproduce, and pass their useful traits along to their offspring. Those organisms that are not well adapted are less likely to survive and reproduce, and the less useful traits die off.

niche: the way an organism fits into an ecosystem.

nocturnal: active at night.

non-avian dinosaurs: dinosaurs that were not birds.

nutrient: a substance in food and soil that living things need to live and grow.

ocean acidification: the process by which the ocean absorbs carbon dioxide from the atmosphere. Through a series of chemical reactions, the ocean becomes more acidic.

organic: of living things, or developing naturally.

organism: any living thing.

over-exploitation: the hunting or taking of a natural resource (such as animals or trees) faster than the population can reproduce, which often leads to extinction.

paleontology: the study of the history of life on Earth. A paleontologist studies paleontology.

Paleozoic Era: a period of time in Earth's history, between 541 and 252 million years ago, when complex forms of life evolved.

period: a division of time within an era.

photosynthesis: the process a plant goes through to make its own food. The plant uses water and carbon dioxide in the presence of sunlight to make oxygen and sugar.

Pleistocene Epoch: a period of time during the Cenozoic Era that lasted from about 2,600,000 years ago to 10,000 years ago.

poaching: the illegal hunting and killing of animals.

pollen: a fine, yellow powder produced by flowering plants. Pollen fertilizes the seeds of other plants as it gets spread around by the wind, birds, and insects.

predator: an animal that hunts another animal for food.

prehistoric: long ago, before written history.

prey: an animal hunted by a predator for food.

primate: any member of a group of animals that includes humans, apes, and monkeys.

primitive: being less developed.

radioactive decay: the process by which the small units that make up an object change and break down.

radioactive element: materials that release their energy and begin to decay.

radiometric dating: a process that measures the decay of radioactive elements, used to determine the age of rocks and fossils.

relative age: the geologic age of rocks or fossils defined by location in the rock strata.

reproduce: to make something new, just like itself. To have babies.

reptile: an animal covered with scales that crawls on its belly or on short legs. Snakes, turtles, and alligators are reptiles.

rewilding: to bring species back to habitats from which they had disappeared.

sanctuary: a safe place.

scavenger: an animal, bird, or insect that eats rotting food or animals that are already dead.

sedimentary rock: rock that is formed by deposits of sediment that settle to the bottom of water and are hardened from pressure.

segmented: divided into parts.

speciation: the evolution of a new species.

species: a group of plants or animals that are closely related and produce offspring.

strata: layers of something.

stratigraphy: the study of the layers of rocks and their relation to geologic time.

sustainable: using natural resources at a rate that allows the resources to recover instead of being wiped out.

swamp: an area of wet, spongy ground that grows woody plants such as trees and shrubs.

tectonic plate: a large section of the earth's crust that moves on top of the mantle, the layer beneath the crust.

theory: an idea that tries to explain why something is the way it is.

theory of evolution: a scientific theory that explains how species change through time and how they have all evolved from simple life forms.

trace fossil: a fossil that is formed from something other than a plant or animal's body, but that shows evidence of life, such as nests, egg shells, poop, burrows, footprints, or leaf impressions.

trilobite: an ancient arthropod that lived during the Paleozoic Era.

trophic cascade: a chain reaction that occurs in an ecosystem when top predators are removed.

tsunami: an enormous ocean wave that is also called a tidal wave.

vaporize: to turn into a gas.

variations: the differences among members of a species.

vertebrate: an animal with a backbone.

viable population: a group with enough individuals to breed and produce offspring so they can maintain their numbers and survive in the wild.

warm-blooded: animals such as humans and bears that can keep themselves warm with their body heat.

Metric Conversions

Use this chart to find the metric equivalents to the English measurements in this book. If you need to know a half measurement, divide by two. If you need to know twice the measurement, multiply by two. How do you find a quarter measurement? How do you find three times the measurement?

English	Metric
1 inch	2.5 centimeters
1 foot	30.5 centimeters
1 yard	0.9 meter
1 mile	1.6 kilometers
1 pound	0.5 kilogram
1 teaspoon	5 milliliters
1 tablespoon	15 milliliters
1 cup	237 milliliters

WEBSITES

The Ocean Through Time – Ocean Portal by the
Smithsonian's National Museum of Natural History
ocean.si.edu/ocean-through-time

PBS – Evolution Library
pbs.org/wgbh/evolution

Galapagos Conservancy
galapagos.org/about_us/about-us

National Geographic – Mission Animal Rescue
kids.nationalgeographic.com/explore/nature/mission-animal-rescue

Radiometric Dating
sciencechannel.com/tv-shows/greatest-discoveries/videos/radiometric-dating

Mass Extinctions Interactive
hhmi.org/biointeractive/mass-extinctions-interactive

Riddle of the Bones
pbs.org/wgbh/evolution/humans/riddle

Becoming Human Documentary
becominghuman.org/node/interactive-documentary

Evolution of Camouflage
rmpbs.pbslearningmedia.org/resource/tdc02.sci.life.evo.camouflage/
evolution-of-camouflage

Arctic Ocean
video.nationalgeographic.com/video/
oceans-narrated-by-sylvia-earle/oceans-arctic

NASA – Climate Kids
climatekids.nasa.gov

Planet Health Report
climatekids.nasa.gov/health-report-temp

Endangered Animals Interactive
sheppardsoftware.com/content/animals/kidscorner/
endangered_animals/overview.htm

MUSEUMS

American Museum of Natural History
New York, New York

University of Michigan Museum of Natural History
Ann Arbor, Michigan

Field Museum of Natural History – *Evolving Planet* exhibit
Chicago, Illinois

Wyoming Dinosaur Center
Thermopolis, Wyoming

Smithsonian's National Museum of Natural History
Washington, D.C.

ANSWER TO
CANINE SKELETAL SYSTEM PROJECT
ON PAGE 12

A dog. Did you figure that out? How?

ESSENTIAL QUESTIONS

Introduction: Should humans try to prevent extinction from happening to existing species? Why or why not?

Chapter 1: What causes a species to go extinct?

Chapter 2: What might life be like on Earth today if the Great Dying hadn't happened?

Chapter 3: What happened to the dinosaurs?

Chapter 4: Is extinction a good thing or a bad thing?

Chapter 5: Why do some species survive while others do not?

Chapter 6: Are we currently experiencing the sixth mass extinction?

Chapter 7: Why is it important to try to change human behavior to save species from going extinct? What can we do to slow extinction rates and the destruction of habitats?

QR CODE GLOSSARY

Page 3: nytimes.com/2012/07/03/science/death-of-lonesome-george-the-tortoise-gives-extinction-a-face.html

Page 19: sharkopedia.discovery.com/shark-topics/prehistoric-sharks/#interactive-timeline-of-shark-evolution

Page 23: fossilpark.org.za/pages/sc-photosyn.html

Page 29: ocean.si.edu/slideshow/foraminifera

Page 29: amnh.org/explore/amnh.tv/(watch)/shelf-life/shelf-life-06-the-tiniest-fossils

Page 39: fossilmuseum.net/index.htm

Page 46: nautil.us/issue/32/space/the-day-the-mesozoic-died

Page 58: tolweb.org/tree

Page 69: bbc.co.uk/timelines/zq8gcdm

Page 85: iucn.org/resources/conservation-tools/iucn-red-list-threatened-species

Page 92: climatekids.nasa.gov

Page 92: www3.epa.gov/carbon-footprint-calculator

Page 100: voices.nationalgeographic.com/2014/02/16/this-will-shatter-your-view-of-apex-predators-how-wolves-change-rivers

Page 104: seafoodwatch.org/seafood-recommendations/our-app

Page 110: joelsartore.com